T0334844

# Informal Empire in Crisis

# Informal Empire in Crisis

British Diplomacy
*and the*
Chinese Customs Succession,
1927-1929

Martyn Atkins

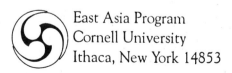
East Asia Program
Cornell University
Ithaca, New York 14853

*The Cornell East Asia Series is published by the Cornell University East Asia Program and is not affiliated with Cornell University Press. We are a small, non-profit press, publishing reasonably priced books on a wide variety of topics relating to East Asia as a service to the academic community and the general public. We accept standing orders which may be cancelled at any time and which provide for automatic billing and shipping of each title in the series upon publication.*

*If after review by internal and external readers a manuscript is accepted for publication, it is published on the basis of camera-ready copy provided by the volume author. Each author is thus responsible for any necessary copy-editing and for manuscript formatting. Submission inquiries should be addressed to Editorial Board, East Asia Program, Cornell University, Ithaca, New York 14853-7601.*

# Contents

# Acknowledgments

My thanks are first due to the Rector and Fellows of Lincoln College, Oxford, who elected me to the Sidgwick Scholarship at Telluride House, thus enabling me to pursue studies leading to the degree of Master of Arts at Cornell University while sharing in the exceptional merits of a unique community. Without the intellectual inspiration and enriching companionship of fellow Telluriders, my time at Cornell would have been far less educational.

My advisors at Cornell—Sherman Cochran, Jeffrey Cody and Charles Peterson—gave freely and generously of their time, expertise and goodwill in bringing an Oxford mediævalist into the domain of modern Chinese history. Ken Pomeranz, Telluride alumnus and a visiting professor at Cornell, made very welcome suggestions on an early draft of the manuscript. Many other Cornell professors, too numerous to thank individually here, ensured that my passage through the unfamiliar territory of American graduate education was as smooth as it was instructive.

In the researches connected with my initial thesis, I was greatly helped by the staff of the British Public Record Office at Kew; the archivist of the School of Oriental and African Studies at the University of London, Mrs. Rosemary Seton; the staff of the SOAS library; the staff of the Oral History Project of the Columbia University Library; and the curator and staff of the Wason Collection of Cornell University Library. My thanks also go to Dr. Robert Bickers, now of Nuffield College, Oxford, whose erudition and expertise, willingly dispensed, did much to put my researches into perspective and provided some valuable leads.

The protracted deliberations which accompanied the transformation of the thesis into a work fit for publication have also been eased by several people: Mrs. Seton at SOAS; the archivist of the Middle East Centre of St. Antony's College, Oxford, Mrs. Diane Ring, and the staff of the Private Papers section there; Mr. Eugene Byrne, who kindly lent me a copy of his dissertation on the dismissal of Sir Francis Aglen; and Dr. Hannah Barker, who kindly—but firmly—read the final proofs. I am also indebted to the most helpful comments and advice of Lord Killearn.

Many persons and presses have given their permission for works in their possession to be reproduced here. The diaries of Miles Lampson, first Baron Killearn, are now lodged at St. Antony's College, Oxford, and excerpts from them appear by the kind permission of the present Lord Killearn. Quotations from the oral memoir of Chang Fu-yun appear by courtesy of The Bancroft Library of the University of California at Berkeley. All quotations from documents held in the possession of the Public Record Office are Crown Copyright, as is the excerpt from Sir Miles Lampson's summary of events in China from 1926 to 1933, which is reproduced on page 105 with the permission of the Controller of Her Majesty's Stationery Office. The extracts from Wm. Roger Louis, *British Strategy in the Far East 1919–1939* (1971) which are quoted on pages 3, 10, 11 and 21 appear by permission of Oxford University Press. The extract from Marie-Claire Bergère, which appears on page 75, was originally published in France in *L'âge d'or de la bourgeoisie chinoise* by Flammarion (1986) and © Editions Flammarion 1986; it was first published in English by Editions de la Maison des Sciences de l'Homme and Cambridge University Press (1989) in *The Golden Age of the Chinese Bourgeoisie 1911–1937*. The English translation is © Maison des Sciences de l'Homme and Cambridge University Press 1989. The quotation on page 23 is reprinted with permission from *Diplomacy and Enterprise: British China Policy 1933–37* by Stephen Lyon Endicott (Vancouver: University of British Columbia Press, 1975), and all rights thereto are reserved by the Publisher. All reasonable efforts have been made to contact the copyright-holders of other published quotations. As some publishers have failed to respond to requests for publication, I have been obliged to resort to the doctrine of 'fair use' in the case of some quotations.

My concluding graces are reserved for the Middle Common Rooms of Lincoln and St. John's Colleges, in whose computer rooms most of this work was revised; for Alice Sheppard, who saw the thesis in the messiest stages of its creation; and for Louise, and Barry, Margaret and Lucy, whose love and support have, as always, made all the difference.

# Abbreviations

| | |
|---|---|
| *AP* | Papers of Sir Francis Aglen |
| *BDRC* | *Biographical Dictionary of Republican China* |
| *CWR* | *China Weekly Review* |
| *DBFP* | *Documents on British Foreign Policy* |
| *FO* | Great Britain, Foreign Office |
| *JSSP* | Papers of John Swire & Son Ltd. |
| *KD* | Diaries of Miles Lampson, first Baron Killearn |
| *MP* | Papers of Sir Frederick Maze |
| *NCH* | *North-China Herald* |
| *NCDN* | *North-China Daily News* |

# Preface

This monograph was inspired by the discovery of a voluminous set of microfilm records which purported to record the official career of a British employee of the governments of republican China. Its documentation of the work of Frederick Maze appeared to tell a fascinating story. At first sight, Maze seemed to be a man locked in a constant battle with the forces of official and unofficial British opinion, fighting for credibility and facing vilification in the name of a just cause. However, the tale which the records told had to be approached with circumspection. Maze's papers are for the most part so wonderfully organised, neatly connecting one set of issues with the next, that one wonders whether the volumes were prepared as part of an attempt at self-vindication. Maze is present throughout the volumes, entering acerbic and barely legible explicatory marginalia followed by his ubiquitous monogram. While the elements of the case he presents may ring true, therefore, one has to be wary of excessive guidance by his insistent hand.

Documentary problems also arise in the assessment of another major corpus of source material. Upon the reorganisation of the Peking Legation dossiers, in May 1927, all files of the series FO 228 dealing with the Customs issue were consigned to dossier 5A or its subsidiaries. While I have nothing but admiration for Archibald Cox, the then Legation archivist, who unwittingly eased my task by confining my researches to this single dossier series, pressure of time prevented me from trawling other likely files in order to collect background evidence. The Foreign Office files dealing with the case operate under a different indexing system, since the compilation of which several files appear to have fallen victims to the practice of 'weeding'. As filing clerks and historians do not necessarily place the same value upon apparently superfluous files, it is quite possible that an amount of useful information may have been lost. Nevertheless, the internal corroboration of both Foreign Office and Legation files is sound enough to confirm the conclusions which I have drawn from the available evidence.

This work is one which relies very much upon epistolary material, the better to comprehend the motivations of the people responsible for China policy and Chinese institutions in the 1920s. Some quotations 'speak with forked tongue', while others appear to twist their readings at will. I have nevertheless tried to assess the particular context in which each comment appears and faithfully to transpose it to the useful support of my argument, on the grounds that paraphrase is a poor and monochromatic device for the expression of the views of others.

I am aware that substantial work has already been performed on my subject, and that the battle between Edwardes and Maze forms the subject-matter of one chapter of Dr. Jean Aitcheson's dissertation on the development of the Chinese Maritime Customs Service.[1] I was careful to guard against the subliminal incorporation of her argument here, although I have since checked her conclusions against my own. This work is in any event less a detailed treatment of the development of the Customs as an institution than a survey of some attitudes of foreigners closely concerned with the future of the Chinese Republic during the Nationalist revolution. Any similarities between the two studies may well stem from a reliance upon many of the same sources rather than any deliberate attempts on my part to follow Dr. Aitcheson's lead.

Dealing with the nationalist movement in 1920s China requires the careful usage of correct terminology. I have tried to be as consistent as possible in referring to the intellectual and popular movement which stemmed from outrage at the continued foreign presence in China as "the nationalist movement," while I refer to the specific manifestation of the principles of nationalism in the Kuomintang and the governments it formed as "the Nationalists," or "the Nationalist government," or sometimes "the South." The Wade-Giles orthographic system is favoured over *pinyin* for reasons of consistency and accuracy in quotation. Calculations of rates of exchange are made on the basis of the table contained in Hsiao Liang-lin, *China's Foreign Trade Statistics, 1864-1949*, pp. 190-92.

---

[1] Jean Aitcheson, *The Chinese Maritime Customs in the Transition from the Ch'ing to the Nationalist Era: An Examination of the Relationship between a Western-style Fiscal Institution and Chinese Government in the Period before the Manchurian Incident.* Unpublished Ph.D. dissertation, Modern History, University of London School of Oriental and African Studies, 1983, ch. 9.

# 1

# The Nature of Informal Empire

The post-colonial desire to comprehend the motivations and impulses which led European states to expand beyond their borders has generated a number of hypotheses regarding the power of such empires to influence other civilisations and political cultures in their own interests. A major contribution to this field of research has been made in the work of John Gallagher and Ronald Robinson, who set out to demolish the notion that imperialism was rampant only in periods of blatant territorial expansion by the colonising nation.[1] With the caveat that "the imperial historian . . . is very much at the mercy of his own particular concept of empire,"[2] they attempted to demonstrate how the policy of the British Empire was largely driven by a prevalent ethic of free trade. If in fact mid-Victorian politicians and civil servants professed to find the idea of formal imperial expansion abhorrent, clinging instead to the view that the source of British prosperity was to be found in the freedom to trade, they nevertheless developed strategies to safeguard and maximise that freedom. As the authors put it, "refusals to annex are no proof of reluctance to control."[3]

While the global theory of 'informal empire' thus presented may since have foundered on regional specificities, it is clear that in China the desire for free trade directly influenced the creation of a foreign establishment which possessed the mentality, if not the coercive power, of a colonial elite. By the turn of the nineteenth century Britain had acquired direct control over nothing more than two tiny parcels of land in Shantung and Kwangtung. Yet by the terms of the various treaties which established foreign rights in China, British businessmen acquired the right freely to trade in the ports thus opened to foreign shipping, and gradually extended their commercial penetration down the South China coast and the Yangtze

---

[1] John Gallagher and Ronald Robinson, "The Imperialism of Free Trade", *Economic History Review* 2nd. series, vol. VI no. 1 (January 1953), pp. 1-15.
[2] *Ibid.*, p. 1.
[3] *Ibid.*, p. 3.

Valley.[4] The general belief that the Chinese judicial and taxational system in the provinces was hopelessly corrupt led the powers who represented such business interests to demand their exemptions from Chinese taxes and jurisdiction. The extraterritorial status thus acquired by foreign citizens in China represented, in theory, a means whereby the freedom to trade equitably on Western terms was protected. In practice the governments representing these citizens were involved in a continual struggle to maintain this freedom, leading in turn to evident and flagrant encroachments upon the sovereignty of the Chinese.[5]

A survey of the studies of British informal empire in 1920s China reveals a basic agreement on the existence of a parasitical foreign establishment. However, opinions differ on the motivation which Britain had and the rationalisations which the British government employed in the defence of such interests. Edmund Fung, for example, takes a broadly strategic view of Britain's interests in South China and the government's attempt to relinquish them with dignity in the heat of the nationalist revolution.[6] Once Chinese nationalists had grasped the effectiveness of the economic weapons of the strike and the boycott over the hopelessness of challenging the powers in diplomacy or war, Britain had to act to maintain the basis of her economic interests in the Far East.[7] Although these interests were less significant in terms of the domestic economy than in terms of the regional predominance they symbolised, Britain still had the "greatest single economic stake in China," and a strong commercial and business lobby both in London and in Shanghai demanded that it be maintained. In Fung's opinion, the Foreign Office felt this could only be maintained by coming to a compromise with the demands of Chinese nationalism and promising to review the so-called 'Unequal Treaties'. While hailing the essential progressiveness of the policy of retreat, he nevertheless finds it "dictated by self-interest, tangible and material objectives."[8] Conciliation with the Chinese was designed to defend as much of the British stake in China as possible by removing the coercive structures which made British trade intolerable to nationalist sentiment. The policy of retreat was also designed

---

[4]*Inter alia* the Treaty of Nanking, 1842; the Treaty of Tientsin, 1858 and the Treaty of Peking, 1860.
[5]A detailed analysis of the effect of informal empire in twentieth-century China is found in Jürgen Osterhammel, "Semi-Colonialism and Informal Empire in Twentieth-Century China: Towards a Framework of Analysis", in Wolfgang J. Mommsen and Jürgen Osterhammel eds., *Imperialism and After: Continuities and Discontinuities* (London: The German Historical Institute; Allen and Unwin, 1986), pp. 290-314.
[6]Edmund S.K. Fung, *The Diplomacy of Imperial Retreat: Britain's South China Policy, 1924–1931* (Hong Kong: Oxford University Press, 1991).
[7]*Ibid.*, pp. 3-6.
[8]*Ibid.*, pp. 8-9.

to renew British prestige in the region, while setting a lead for other powers to follow. Fung gives by far the most detailed published treatment of British policy over this period. In dealing with the discussions and debates of British diplomats and Foreign Office officials, he succeeds both in conveying the idea that the 'informal empire' was tangible and worth defending and in demonstrating the apparent rationality and good faith of those entrusted with carrying out the policy of retreat. Yet it is only in conclusion that he deals with the limitations of Britain's approach to the developing Chinese nation: "a policy of circumspection and restraint which betrayed an attitude of affable condescension combined with mistrustful disdain."[9] The logic of this strategy, then, was predicated not only on British interests, but also on the British conception of the capabilities of the Chinese. Seen in relation to the formal structures of diplomacy, the British approach to Chinese nationalism may well appear particularly liberal. Yet the personal reactions of some British diplomats to the actions of Chinese politicians and officials, and indeed the Chinese as a race, reveal deep-seated prejudices which tended to dilute the overall effectiveness of British overtures.

In this regard, Roger Louis' survey on the British approach to the Far East between the wars acts as a useful complement to Fung's work.[10] While this treatment of the subject is more impressionistic than that of Fung, and its canvas broader, it nevertheless makes a stronger argument for an analysis of racial attitudes as they underlay British policy towards China. His attempt to "illuminate the preconceptions or set of often unstated assumptions about Asia which British statesmen brought with them as they tried to cope with Japan or China" explores the effect of individual personalities on British strategy, as well as stressing the necessity of accounting for contemporary theories of race and colour as they appeared in the intellectual baggage of British statesmen and diplomats.[11] This provides a useful complement to the Gallagher-Robinson theory of informal empire: if there existed an institutional sophistry which permitted diplomatic coercion in the pursuit of 'free' trade, it is reasonable to assume that its practitioners operated under a set of assumptions which may appear unpalatable or illogical to post-colonial researchers. The idea that even the most enlightened British diplomats of the age had an underlying belief in the racial character of nations should initiate a reassessment of the stated willingness of Britain to withdraw from its informal commitments in China. Louis reminds the reader

---

[9]*Ibid.*, p. 246.
[10]Wm. Roger Louis, *British Strategy in the Far East 1919–1939* (Oxford: Clarendon Press, 1971).
[11]*Ibid.*, pp. 1-3.

that individuals make and influence policy in pursuit of a national interest, and that the historian of colonial relations cannot afford to ignore the psychological ramifications of perceived difference on the development of such policy.

There is an inherent danger in this approach in that one may use theory as a convenient substitute for a thorough analysis of the complexity of the historical record. Yet to deny an element of individual or collective racial prejudice in the defence of British interests in the 1920s is to present a view of great-power diplomacy perhaps more enlightened than any established before or since. If one remembers that the premises for the establishment of extraterritoriality, the main prop of informal empire and its manifestation most hateful to the Chinese, was that foreign nationals would be unable to receive just and fair treatment in China without its protection, then one realises the intractability of the issue; if the Chinese *as a race* were considered incapable of moral and upright behaviour as judged by Western standards, then the reaction of Britons dealing with Chinese would be permanently influenced by this perception, irrespective of individual attempts to achieve a *rapprochement*.

As a general statement, this is perhaps a fair characterisation of the basic problem which underlay the foreign presence in the Far East. Nicholas Clifford nevertheless demonstrates how easy it is to adopt an overly general view of such foreign prejudices.[12] The encapsulating phrases "the Shanghai Mind" and "Old China hands" have been susceptible to application without particular reference to precise definition, historical moment or circumstantial nuance. Are the "Old China Hands" those late nineteenth-century *taipans* of Nathan Pelcovits' study, who earned their reputation by ceaselessly badgering the Foreign Office into aggressive action to protect trade in China?[13] Or are they the representatives of British commercial houses in China in the 1920s, disdainful of the manner in which their forebears had antagonised the Chinese and demanding that the Foreign Office act either to conciliate or to remove the nationalist threat?[14] Similarly, when one talks of the "Shanghai Mind," is one addressing the hideous xenophobia in its foreign community which Arthur Ransome chronicled for the *Manchester Guardian* in 1927, or is one invoking the well-meaning condescension,

---

[12]Nicholas R. Clifford, "A Revolution Is Not a Tea Party: The "Shanghai Mind(s)" Reconsidered", *Pacific Historical Review* vol. 59 no. 4 (November 1990), pp. 501-26.

[13]Nathan A. Pelcovits, *Old China Hands and the Foreign Office* (New York: American Institute of Foreign Relations; King's Crown Press, 1948).

[14]Fung, *op. cit.*, p. 242-43: Fung concludes that the Foreign Office held out against the pressure to crush the Nationalists and made no concessions to the business lobby. As I shall briefly indicate below, there was a pragmatic element in the business community which aimed, however misguidedly, to come to terms with some of the issues of Chinese nationalism.

which Clifford identifies, towards the Chinese ability to develop upon Western lines?[15]

Taking into account the difficulties of generalisation, it is possible to demonstrate that the attitudes delineated in the above cases, and many others, are the product of an attempt by foreigners to make sense of their presence in China. In the light of the overthrow of the Manchu dynasty, the decline of British global power and the rise of Chinese nationalism, the predominantly British foreign community of 1920s Shanghai was forced to cast around for excuses for the continued existence of extraterritorial jurisdiction. Clifford shows how the nationalist movement was countered by the "diehard" section of the community, which maintained that since the foreign presence in China was beneficial to the Chinese nation, "anti-foreignism" and nationalism were simply incompatible.[16] Yet there were other, more carefully elaborated responses, which each in their own way attempted to come to terms with the considerable cultural disjunctions with which Britons were faced.

For example, the correspondence between the directors of John Swire and Sons indicates a genuine effort to limit the excesses of the Shanghai diehards and to achieve some form of working relationship with the Chinese.[17] One Swire director travelled east each year to supervise the activities of Butterfield and Swire, the umbrella company for Swire's Chinese shipping, trading and sugar-refining interests. The reports sent home are generally concerned with the deleterious effect of anti-foreign agitation on Swire's trading, particularly in 1926 when the entire Upper Yangtze fleet of the China Navigation Company was laid up due to such unrest. The problems which taxed the directors generally concerned the means of coming to some form of accommodation with Chinese nationalism, which would, it was recognised, in all probability carry the day. Warren Swire advocated a forthright attempt to capture the high ground:

> In view of the probable future, when the Chinese will have a large if not the dominant voice in the administration of many areas of foreign residence all over the country . . . it will obviously be to the

---

[15]Arthur Ransome, *The Chinese Puzzle* (London: George Allen and Unwin, 1927), pp. 28-32: Clifford, *op. cit.*, pp. 517-22. A similar approach to the American communities of Shanghai may be found in James Layton Huskey, "The Cosmopolitan Connection: Americans and Chinese in Shanghai during the Interwar Years", *Diplomatic History* vol. 11 no. 3 (Summer 1987), pp. 227-43.

[16]*Ibid.*, pp. 506-12.

[17]*The Papers of John Swire and Sons Ltd (JSSP)*, in particular Additional Box 15, Personal Letters from Managers to Directors, 1925–1930.

advantage of these foreigners themselves that these men should have had a proper training, whilst foreigners still had the deciding voice.[18]

Swire advocated a concerted campaign to educate Chinese students, "bringing the latter into actual contact with the facts, as we see them." While such a policy was clearly aimed at making 'intellectual compradors', it demonstrated a recognition that Chinese nationalism was to be accommodated and not dismissed. Swire wanted a thorough renewal of the company's attitude towards dealing with Chinese staff and merchants: he described the need for the head of the China Navigation Company's Shanghai department to have "the political sense, which understands and acts on the present need for cultivating in and out of office and so educating Chinese shipowners and business men."[19] Some employees had this knack, others did not. For example, a certain manager was "much too direct . . . when he caught a Chinese out in a misstatement, he called it straight off a damned lie, instead of asking politely, whether there was not some misunderstanding."[20] There was thus a growing appreciation of the cultural and linguistic accomodations to be made for the more effective conduct of business on Chinese terms. Jock Swire advocated a reform of the language course established for the training of company 'griffins' who were destined to rise to high management positions, abandoning the old office-based examination system in favour of a programme of cultural immersion in Nanking or Peking along the lines of the successful scheme run by the British-American Tobacco Company.[21] Directors also encouraged a concerted effort towards establishing social contacts with Chinese politicians and businessmen: "this is important, since so much will depend in the future on personal acquaintance and even intimacy with the political as well as the merchant clique."[22]

---

[18]*JSSP* add. 15: letter out from G.W.S[wire] (London) to C.C.S[cott] (Shanghai) of 22 October 1926.
[19]*JSSP* add. 15: letter out from G.W.S[wire] (London) to J.K.S[wire] (China) of 2 May 1930.
[20]*Ibid.*
[21]'Griffin' was an epithet applied to the young and promising recruits to foreign companies in the East recently arrived in China. Jock Swire first mentions a reform of the language-training scheme in order to inculcate some "Chinese atmosphere" in April 1930: *JSSP* add. 15: letter from J. K. S[wire] (Shanghai) to J[ohn] S[wire] & S[ons] (London) of 18 April 1930.
[22]In December 1927 Swire's London office suggested to the Shanghai managers that the best venues for conducting such entertainments, and the ones which had the most desirable diplomatic *cachet*, were the managers' own homes, rather than the hackneyed Union Club: *JSSP* II 2/6 (box 42), p. 38(c): inter-office letter from London to Shanghai of 16 December 1927. In 1929 Warren Swire declared that the function of the official residence of the Shanghai manager was "not to entertain foreign society, but the Chinese political and economic magnates, who require something good." He found that those entertained there, such as former Deputy Minister of Finance Quo Tai-chi and chairmen K.P. Chen of the Shanghai Commercial

It should not be supposed that these apparently progressive attitudes were in any way the manifestations of a spirit of altruism or represented the fullest concession possible to the spirit of the nationalist revolution. Rather, they represented an astute attempt by Swire's management to co-opt the spirit of the nationalist movement, the better to avoid future damaging conflicts. Warren Swire was convinced of the capacity of the British China trader to come to a mutually beneficial arrangement with the Chinese, and had harsh words for the "defeatist rabbits" in the Shanghai commercial community and the diplomatic and consular corps alike:

> Shai [Shanghai] drives me to despair. They must read the writing on the wall, they are self-satisfied, they are defeatist & they have no FAITH. China depends in the last resort & perhaps all the way through on Faith in our destiny. . . . They don't realise that there is more to business than cash & I believe that young China expects more from the foreigner than a mere mutual desire to make money.[23]

The perspectives of British traders and British diplomats were thus not necessarily consonant. Swire's directors routinely criticised the British Legation and the Foreign Office for taking a passive stance on Chinese issues. Jock Swire was scathing about an encounter he had had with Sydney Mayers, sometime director of the British and Chinese Railways Corporation:

> We dined one night with Sir Ernest Wilton; I sat next [to] S. Mayers who turned to me very gloomily at the soup & in his most pompous & pontifical manner said:- " I want you to give Warren a serious message from me; 'Get out of China, it is Ichabod. You will get no help from home & will go the way of the merchants in Smyrna. We came to China with the sword & gun in our hands & until the Washington Conference we remained here by the sword; the Chinese never asked us to come, they never wanted us, they don't want us now. Realizing during the last few months that we have seriously and finally put away the sword they have made up their minds to get rid of us and they will do it. They may do it in my life-time, they will certainly do it in yours. Shape your whole policy to get out of China; it is Ichabod.'" This from one in constant touch with the British Empire's representatives is most encouraging!! He continued in the same pessimistic attitude the whole evening so you can imagine we

---

and Savings Bank and Li Ming of the Chekiang Industrial Bank "have . . . more to talk about than the foreigners here." *JSSP* add. 15: letter from G. W. S[wire] (Shanghai) to unidentified recipient, undated (sequentially in early 1929).

[23] *JSSP* add. 15: letter from G.W.S[wire] (Peking) to J.K S[wire] (London) of 23 February 1929.

had a pretty cheerful party but when you see the hopeless atmosphere of fatuous note-writing to Chinese Ministers who probably don't exist in which he lives, it is not surprising. The Legation will not adapt their machinery to present conditions but still carry on quite gaily as though they were in Paris or Berlin dealing with an efficient Government. I told him that I had realised for five years that our own Government was 'Ichabod' but that that fortunately did not necessarily mean that we must get out of China.[24]

There were also differences of opinion within the British diplomatic establishment as to how to handle the Chinese, derived in part from the divided nature of the service. British consuls in China were initially recruited specifically to serve in China as student interpreters; they made their way through the consular ranks, aspiring to the charge of a major treaty-port such as Shanghai or Canton, or to a transfer into the Diplomatic Service. By virtue of their role as the immediate guardians of the principle of extraterritoriality, consuls were often highly vulnerable in the face of nationalist onslaughts, holding as they did the ultimate jurisdiction over British subjects accused of crimes committed in China.[25] A rigid hierarchy also prevented some promising candidates from making full use of their talents through early promotion into those positions of responsibility which called for men especially sensitive to the vagaries of the Chinese political situation. In early 1928 a Swire director, H.W. Robertson, suggested that the company might offer the Canton Consul, John Brenan, a high-ranking position in Swire's "diplomatic and intelligence work," perhaps as the Swire nominee to the Shanghai Municipal Council. Brenan was due to go on leave, and it was felt that his chances of early promotion to a better position on his return were slim given his relative youth (he was forty-four) and the restrictions of "Service conditions and tradition." Robertson thought that Brenan's low seniority would entitle him at best to the charge of a minor port such as Amoy. Warren Swire had misgivings about the virtue in "tempting" Brenan from British service, but he also held that a Swire job would be more appealing and challenging. In February 1929 he asked Sir Miles Lampson, British Minister in Peking, "how did [he] feel about private firms offering lucrative jobs to men in the Consular Service" (i.e. Brenan): Lampson was less than sanguine about Brenan's prospects for promotion,

---

[24]*JSSP* add. 15: letter from J.K.S[wire] (s.s. 'Huichow') to G.W.S[wire] (London) of 19 June 1925. Ichabod was the posthumous son of Phinehas and grandson of Eli, both killed in the Philistine capture of the Ark of the Covenant (1 Sam. iv): his name translates as "no glory" (*Brewer's Dictionary of Phrase and Fable*, 2nd. revised edn.)

[25]For a detailed treatment of the Consular Service in China, see P.D. Coates, *The China Consuls: British Consular Officers, 1843–1943* (Hong Kong: Oxford University Press, 1988).

but was loth to lose such an able consul.[26] When, however, Brenan was unexpectedly appointed Shanghai Consul-General later in 1929, the situation was resolved to the benefit of both parties.[27]

It would be impossible to stereotype the attitudes of consuls to Chinese service. On the one extreme there stood the sometime darling of the Shanghai diehards, Sidney Barton, whose staunch refusal to cooperate with the independent inquiry into the May 30th Incident of 1925, in which British policemen opened fire on a Chinese demonstration, earned him a certain notoriety both in Peking and London.[28] On the other there stood men such as Meyrick Hewlett, a veteran of the Boxer Uprising whose memoir is peppered with sentimental references to the simplicity of the "humble" Chinese.[29] Hewlett served as consul at Chengtu, Amoy and Nanking during the 1920s, and was at one point invited to be Chinese Secretary at the Legation, an offer never confirmed.[30] His appreciation of Chinese culture, though simplistic, was genuine:

> I do not believe that if you speak Chinese you of necessity become less and less English. Neither do I believe that if you write Chinese your mentality has become such that you are perhaps not quite normal. Rather do I feel that by speaking Chinese you can get to the heart of the people, by writing you win their innermost thoughts.[31]

That Hewlett felt obliged to pen such lines perhaps indicates a defensive reaction to a particularly vicious manifestation of British xenophobia. He would, however, be considered somewhat archaic in his attitudes today: his professed admiration for the Chinese overflows with patronising references, and although he has some appreciation for the efforts of the Nanking Government, whose operations he witnessed at first hand, he despairs of the ability of any Chinese government to muster the "higher virtues" of patriotism and efficiency which he feels necessary: " . . . not until the highest in the land realise the true meaning of Public SERVANT will China fulfil the magnificent destiny which is hers."[32]

---

[26]*Killearn Diaries*, f. 25r (1929): February 25th 1929.

[27]*JSSP* add. 15: letter from H.W. R[obertson] (Hong Kong) to J[ohn] S[wire] & S[ons] (London) of 13 January 1928: reply from G.W. S[wire] of 24 February 1928.

[28]Nicholas R. Clifford, *Spoilt Children of Empire: Westerners in Shanghai and the Chinese Revolution of the 1920's* (Hanover, N.H.: Middlebury College Press; University Press of New England, 1991), pp. 121-22.

[29]Sir Meyrick Hewlett, *Forty Years in China* (London: Macmillan & Co, 1944).

[30]*Ibid.*, p. 150. The inference to be drawn from this refusal was that the new Minister, Sir Ronald Macleay, who took over in 1922, had failed to confirm the appointment made by his predecessor, Sir Beilby Alston.

[31]*Ibid.*, p. 250.

[32]*Ibid.*, p. 258.

Other consuls were decidedly more frank about the shortcomings of Chinese in public life. H.F. Handley-Derry, Consul at Chungking, wrote in 1928 to the British Legation concerning the Acting Commissioner of Customs, Chow Tzu-ching, who wanted a foreign commissioner appointed to succeed him:

> The conditions are becoming better, but that is not the reason why Chow wants a foreigner, the reason is he finds himself, I feel sure, often in difficult situations by reason merely that he is a Chinese, and cannot take up a line of action with the officials with any hope of success. Very often an official will put forward a proposition merely because he has been asked to do so by some other official, and because he does not feel he can refuse without some good reason. If either of the officials felt there would be effective opposition put forward with good reasons to support it, they would be only too pleased, but with the moral flabbiness of the Chinese mind, they are not prepared to take the responsibility themselves.[33]

Justifications for the foreign presence in China continued at the level of the Legation. Eric Teichman, the official selected instead of Hewlett to fill the position of Chinese Secretary, was moved in 1937 to write an exposition of Chinese affairs relating to the development of the conflict with Japan.[34] He was more usefully analytical than Hewlett about the strategic reasons for the British presence, and Louis hails his work as "one of the most important British memoirs on China."[35] Teichman provides a reasoned viewpoint which concedes to Chinese nationalism a fair amount of moral high ground, while unapologetically maintaining the need for a continued British presence. Britons might have wronged the Chinese nation in the past and unnecessarily sown jealousy and discord—Teichman is particularly scathing towards the "old die-hard 'China Hand' "—but in general the British pursuit of trade in China had only been to China's benefit.

> Britain has dealt fairly and justly by China; and the Chinese historian of the future may well write down Great Britain as China's best and oldest friend. In all its ups-and-downs British policy has always first and last aimed at the furtherance of British trade; and to this end

---

[33]FO 228/3741/5A/96 1928: letter from Handley-Derry (Chungking) to Lampson of 13 June 1928.

[34]Sir Eric Teichman, *Affairs of China: A Survey of the Recent History and Present Circumstances of the Republic of China* (London: Methuen, 1938). He points out (p. 287) that the Chinese Secretary and Secretariat were officially departments of the Consular Service, but working so closely with the Legation as to be inseparable.

[35]Louis, *op. cit.*, p. 277.

sought always to promote a prosperous, united and independent China.

That the Chinese have at times had reason to be irritated at and impatient with British policy cannot be denied. But the British Government have realized the need of moving with the times; and insist only that the changes as they affect British interests should be gradual and evolutionary. On both sides old prejudices are disappearing amongst the younger generation.[36]

The desire for accommodation with Chinese nationalism thus had some important and influential advocates in the British commercial and diplomatic establishments in China, even though the evidence of such advocacy in some cases appeared only after events made it justifiable. Moreover, accommodation was partially hampered by the persistent exasperation which arose when Chinese politicians and officials resolutely refused to conform to Western ideas on the practice of responsible government. Even Lampson, British Minister from 1926 to 1933 and a man praised by Fung for his skilful orchestration of the British retreat, occasionally lost patience. Writing on the proposed sinification of the Chinese Maritime Customs in 1929, he declared " . . . if the Chinese were normal people who could safely be given positions of responsibility and trust I would have less hesitation [about sinification] than I have!"[37]

The continuing attempts of well-meaning Europeans to make sense of their role in China should not necessarily be dismissed out of hand. Louis, citing Jean Stengers, defends the value of a historicist approach: " . . . if there is an important connection between historical truth and psychological truth, then it is important to comprehend how men understood events of the time in order to understand the meanings of the events themselves."[38] One might deride such efforts to come to terms with nationalist China as hopeless and patronising, the defence of the indefensible. This would be a reasonable approach if one were interested in providing a blanket indictment of the foreign presence in China. For example, Roberta Dayer condemns the activities of the China Consortium and the Foreign Office in the 1920s as operating simply as tools of the Anglo-American financial establishment, intent on exploiting China to the utmost under the pretence of developing her infrastructure. She criticises Louis' concentration on race to the exclusion of

---

[36]Teichman, *op. cit.*, pp. 50-51.
[37]Fung, *op. cit.*, pp. 245-46. FO 228/3943/5A/34 1929: Lampson minute to Maze report on sinification, 6 July 1929.
[38]Louis, *op. cit.*, p. 3.

the theme of "economic exploitation which that racism facilitated."[39] Greed, in Dayer's view, predominated as the defining characteristic of British policy, and co-opted racial arguments as justification for further exploitation. This may perhaps have been true in the arid political arenas where such agreements were brokered, in the the making of crucial decisions and the public justification of injustice. Yet diplomats and businessmen in China also existed as private citizens in a strange and increasingly hostile land. When anti-foreign demonstrations put men in fear of their lives, it was surely not greed which motivated them to reassess and rationalise their relationships with the Chinese to the point of contemplating retreat.

It is not my intention here to enter into detailed debates about the aims, motives and effects of the foreign presence. What I have tried to do instead is to illuminate some of the personal dilemmas and contradictions of the representatives of British concerns in China: the 'men on the spot', as Christopher Bowie, among others, has termed them.[40] Variously required by government, public opinion or shareholders to come to some accommodation with the difference of the Chinese, their preconceptions invariably prevented them from achieving a fully satisfactory result. My contention is that the foreigner in Nationalist China, surrounded by injustice and set about by hostile forces, had a choice to make, whether consciously or unconsciously motivated: he could stand firm for what he perceived as the values of the West against the apparent indolence and corruption of the Chinese, or he could come to an understanding of China's drive for nationhood and approach it in a spirit of partnership rather than hostility. While to cast all foreigners into these two broad groups is necessarily to do injustices to some, the issues resolve themselves along these lines with apparent ease in the narrative upon which this monograph hangs. It is now not at all easy to justify the foreign presence in China from first principles: yet the ingenious attempts of many Westerners to make the best of a slow and inevitable retreat invite closer attention.

---

[39]Roberta Allbert Dayer, *Bankers and Diplomats in China 1917–1925: The Anglo-American Relationship* (London: Frank Cass, 1981), pp. xxiii-xxiv.
[40]Christopher John Bowie, *Great Britain and the Use of Force in China 1919–1931*, unpublished D.Phil. dissertation, Modern History, University of Oxford, 1983.

# 2

# Whitehall's Response to Chinese Nationalism

The years from 1925 to 1927 saw Chinese nationalism at its fullest flood, with British interests in China the unwilling target of the rage of agitators. Following the incident of May 30th 1925 in Shanghai, the further shooting of demonstrators at Canton that June initiated a highly damaging strike and boycott of British goods in both Canton and Hong Kong. Britons, both in China and in Whitehall, looked on with impotent horror as the Kremlin and the Kuomintang appeared to grow ever closer, and as the agitational propaganda of the former took a greater hold on the imagination of anti-imperialist mobs. Direct threats to British lives and property challenged the basis of the British presence in China and struck at the fundamental assumptions which sustained the informal empire.

The movement against British interests was motivated as much by the language of symbolism as by the practicalities of politics. As the main protagonist of the wars of 1842 and 1860, and a major party to the dashing of Chinese hopes of treaty revision at the Treaty of Versailles, Britain was the principal target of anti-foreign agitation. The British Minister, Sir Ronald Macleay, had railed in vain against the apparently unfair caricature of Britons as arch-imperialists, and vehemently denounced the Soviet Union for its sponsorship of a campaign of anti-foreign hatred. Meanwhile, the Foreign Office was casting around for a firm policy which would command the support of the eight other signatories to the Washington Treaty. Concluded in 1922, this pact had attempted to mollify Chinese discontent over the disappointments of Versailles by checking Japanese naval expansionism and promising treaty revision once the Republic had taken stable form.[1] It found none, for in the aftermath of the Washington Conference the unanimity of the Powers with respect to Chinese affairs had all but disappeared for want

---

[1] The participants in the Washington Conference of 1921–22 were the British Empire, the United States, France, Italy, Japan, Belgium, the Netherlands, Portugal and Holland. A fuller account is given in Westel W. Willoughby, *China at the Conference: A Report* (Baltimore, Md.: The Johns Hopkins Press, 1922).

of an effective central Chinese government with which binding agreements could be negotiated. The one nation specifically excluded from the family of treaty powers was only too happy to make its own approaches to the Chinese market, unaided by a treaty system which by this time had become as much of an embarrassment as a safeguard. Germany renounced her rights and privileges in China in 1921 and in return gained a degree of respite from the ravages of anti-foreignism. While the flowering of German trade with China would have to wait until the establishment of the Nationalist regime, its first shoots were seen in Canton during the anti-British boycott.[2]

One of the most pressing problems confronting foreign interests in China concerned tariff revenue. In 1925 the revenue which nominally accrued to the Peking government from the collection of duty on internal and external trade amounted to over seventy million Haikwan taels, or just under sixty million U.S. dollars at the prevailing rate of exchange. This sum was the product of a combined import and export balance of 1.7 billion Haikwan taels, over forty percent of which was due to trade passing through the port of Shanghai. Whether the Peking government was to be granted the authority to collect more tariff revenue in the form of a 2½ per cent surtax upon the five per cent duty *ad valorem* already permitted had greatly troubled the powers at Washington, not least because it had become more difficult to take Peking's claims upon the whole of the revenue seriously.[3]

Britain had hoped that the Peking Tariff Conference of 1925-26 would yield a new consensus on the division of tariff revenues within China by allocating the Customs surtax revenues provisionally granted in 1922 by the Washington Conference to the authorities controlling the provinces in which they were collected. This was a solution which would mollify the Canton government while relieving Britain of the obligation of having to deal with it directly. Yet the Conference proved inconclusive, the plan failed, and all that was granted was the promise to give a central Chinese government autonomy over the setting of tariffs by 1929. By the summer of 1926 the lack of a clear China policy had had such a deleterious effect on commercial confidence and Britain's international prestige that the Foreign Office was forced to search in radically new directions, even at the expense of breaking ranks with the other treaty powers.[4]

---

[2]For an analysis of the success of German trade with China between the wars, see William C. Kirby, *Germany and Republican China* (Stanford, Calif.: Stanford University Press, 1984), especially p. 24.

[3]Data on trade and Customs figures are taken from tables in Hsiao Liang-lin, *China's Foreign Trade Statistics 1864–1949* (Cambridge, Mass.: East Asian Research Center, Harvard University, 1974), especially pp. 24, 131 and 269.

[4]For what follows, the main source is Fung, *op. cit.*, pp. 81-104.

The lines of the new policy were in great measure laid out by two men who had become increasingly restless with Britain's continued failure to address the nationalist cause in China. Sir Victor Wellesley, Under-Secretary of State for Foreign Affairs, was not necessarily sympathetic to the nationalistic aspirations of the Chinese, but was in general not optimistic about Britain's capacity to dominate the Chinese scene as had been the case in the years before the Great War. John Pratt was a member of the Consular Service whose most recent posting had been as Acting Consul-General in Shanghai. He had been seconded to the Department on a one-year rotation as an expert on Chinese affairs, and was retained for the next thirteen. His very definite views on Britain's responsibility towards the nationalist movement were articulated in numerous and exhaustively analytical minutes and memoranda, and his command of the intricacies of the anti-foreign campaign made such observations indispensable. Nevertheless, his official status as a consul on secondment meant that his opinions did not command automatic priority; he had to use his persuasive writing style and his formidable erudition to put across views which others in the Department found to be unacceptably liberal.[5]

Pratt was the son of a colonial officer in British India and his Indian wife. While a half-caste appearance undoubtedly aided one of his brothers, who was to find success in the film industry under the pseudonym Boris Karloff, Pratt's dark complexion had caused him embarrasment in Shanghai and London society. Among his colleagues he was jovially known as "Black Pratt" and "Uncle Tom's Cabin," and while such nicknames may have been good-humoured, they may also have served to heighten Pratt's sensitivities.[6] In Shanghai he had once been thrown out of the Municipal Gardens by a park-keeper unaware of his occupation. Pratt was undoubtedly in a position to empathise with the position of the Chinese in the treaty ports, and was also aware of the patronising assumptions which underlay foreign attitudes towards the Chinese Republic. While Wellesley was of the pragmatic opinion that it was impolitic for Britain to maintain a policy of intervention in China to support its interests, Pratt was intellectually convinced of the eventual necessity of the demolition of the treaty regime. The conviction of the right of the Chinese people to equality in the family of nations, and,

---

[5]For the Far Eastern Department reorganisation the source is William James Megginson III, *Britain's Response to Chinese Nationalism, 1925–1927: The Foreign Office Search for a New Policy*, unpublished Ph.D. dissertation, History, George Washington University, 1973, pp. 209-226. For Pratt's position, Ann Trotter, "Backstage Diplomacy: Britian [sic] and Japan in the 1930's", *Journal of Oriental Studies* vol. 15 no. 1 (January 1977), p. 39.

[6]Coates (*The China Consuls*, pp. 429-30) remarks upon the "colour feeling" encountered in the Consular Service by Pratt and another brother, R. S. Pratt, consul at Hoihow and Chungking.

furthermore, of the essential integrity of Chinese society and culture, marked Pratt out as a 'liberal'–or, as William Strang, another Department official, put it, a man with "a touch of the fanatic [who] needs (and gets) the curb."[7]

While Pratt and Wellesley may have differed in their basic opinions of the right of the Chinese to full governmental integrity, they shared a belief that the Nationalist regime would continue to expand its influence. This view was supported by a number of consular despatches from China stations. Even Sidney Barton in Shanghai had come around to the opinion that the Nationalists were "destined to rule China."[8] Clear evidence of Nationalist gains since the launching of the Northern Expedition in February 1926 convinced the Foreign Secretary, Austen Chamberlain, that a means of accommodation with Nationalist politicians had to be found.

This approach challenged the conventional wisdom. Ever since the collapse of the Tariff Conference, Whitehall's supposed weakness on the question of Chinese nationalism had drawn vociferous criticism from the Peking Legation, much of the commercial community in Shanghai and the China lobby in Parliament and outside.[9] Admittedly, those not acquainted with Pratt's insights needed to make something of a leap of faith to depart from the prevailing opinion and to believe that the linkage between Bolshevism and Chinese nationalism was a shaky one. Nevertheless, Pratt's beliefs were supported by Wellesley's conviction that the time when Britain could use force in China to protect her own interests was long past—and furthermore, the Nine-Power Treaty signed at Washington formally prohibited any such course.

The urgency of the situation prompted the Foreign Office to override the advice of the Peking Legation in the formulation of policy, thus departing from normal practice. Although Macleay had shown himself to be sufficiently prejudiced against the Nationalists to be ineffective in any such policy of conciliation, and flatly refused orders to send an envoy to Hankow to liaise with Nationalist leaders, there were still doubts about the wisdom of contradicting the 'man on the spot'.[10] While the imposition of policy from above may have forcibly removed the main sticking-point hindering the development of good relations with the Kuomintang, the manner of its

---

[7]Megginson, *op. cit.,* p. 214.

[8]FO 371/11621: F 513/1/10: "Memo respecting Canton" by Frank Ashton-Gwatkin, 3 February 1926: cited in Fung, *op. cit.,* p. 91.

[9]Louis, *op. cit.,* p. 151. In mid-1926 Lord Southborough formed the China Committee, an association of British business interests which aimed to pressure the Foreign Office into an interventionist China policy. Fung, *op. cit.,* p. 95.

[10]Richard Stremski, *The Shaping of British Policy during the Nationalist Revolution in China* (Taipei: Soochow University Department of Political Science, 1979), p. 102: Fung, *op. cit.,* p. 93.

delivery and the personnel involved in its formulation may not have delighted the hearts of Legation officials, some of whom were also decidedly lukewarm towards Pratt's liberal ideas.

The new policy on China was officially promulgated on 18 December 1926 in the form of a memorandum to the signatories of the Washington treaties. This "December Memorandum" recognised the "legitimate aspirations of the Chinese people," proposed the swift establishment of Chinese tariff autonomy and declared the essential justice of Chinese claims for treaty revision. It expressed the hope that the treaty powers would soon join in this British initiative, showing the spirit of goodwill by softening a strict insistence on treaty rights and moving without delay to grant those Customs surtaxes approved in principle at the Washington Conference.[11] Although Fung argues that in choosing this form of promulgation Britain maintained faith with the spirit of Washington, in actual fact the other treaty powers were distinctly taken aback at this British initiative, coming as it did from a nation in a position of some weakness in China.

Britain had been forced to act in this unilateral fashion because Whitehall's discomfiture had hitherto rather suited the other powers, none of whom had been subjected to such grievous assaults on their trade. It took them rather by surprise: the *Herald Tribune* reported that Paris was "unhesitatingly skeptical," Tokyo "frankly unenthusiastic" and Washington "uncomfortably pleased" with a British policy which appeared to usurp American initiatives on the tariff question.[12] The American Minister, MacMurray, was opposed to the Memorandum on the grounds that it might force the issue on a number of other sensitive subjects, such as extraterritoriality; but the Secretary of State, Frank B. Kellogg, ordered him to support the British initiative as its line on tariff autonomy parallelled that of the State Department.[13] This line was in direct opposition to the Japanese policy of determining strict conditions for the uses of surtax revenues before creating the conditions for further borrowing by Peking upon the security of the revenue these surtaxes might generate.[14] Japan still awaited repayment of the Nishihara loans, contracted with Peking in 1905 and adversely affecting Tokyo's deficit balance, and was thus liable to take a hard line on issues concerning Chinese credit.[15]

Fiscal issues aside, the new British policy which the December Memorandum represented was couched both in terms of conciliation and of

[11]Fung, *op. cit.*, pp. 101-02.
[12]Dorothy Borg, *American Policy and the Chinese Revolution, 1925–1928* (New York: East Asian Institute, Columbia University: Octagon Books, 1968), p. 231.
[13]Borg, *op. cit.*, pp. 231-33.
[14]Akira Iriye, *After Imperialism* (Cambridge, Mass.: Harvard University Press, 1965), p. 100.
[15]*Ibid.*, p. 37.

moral imperatives. Wellesley had said that Britain must "do the right thing by China"[16] and the chief of the Foreign Office Press Bureau told American audiences that:

> . . . as time went on and as it became more and more obvious that it might be at least years before China again acquired an effective central government, and as the nationalist movement gained strength, and as the agitation against the one-sided treaties grew and grew, it began to be felt in London that nothing much could be lost and that something might be gained, certainly morally and perhaps materially, by a gesture on the part of the treaty powers which would prove to the nationalists–and by the nationalists I mean something more than the Southern Government and the followers–that we really meant business at the Washington Conference, that we were not, as the Chinese extremists and their Bolshevik friends were always proclaiming, simply using the impotence of the Peking Government and the general chaos of China as a pretext for delaying concessions which we had never really meant to grant.[17]

Sir Arthur Willert's attempt to expand the scope of the Memorandum to cover all nationalist sentiment disguised the need to come to a speedy accommodation with the Kuomintang while overcoming several years of mutual distrust. There was, moreover, little to lose by strengthening moderate party members in the belief that Britain was serious about treaty revision. Nevertheless, although the Memorandum may have represented, to quote Teichman, "a triumph of enlightened common sense," Fung demonstrates that in fact Britain was promising to concede very little without definite assurances of the future stability of a national Chinese government.[18] Although the promised grant of the Washington surtaxes was made unilaterally by Britain to all Chinese factions in January 1927, the "idealistic rhetoric" of the Memorandum concealed the fact that the ball was now in the Chinese court. The future success of the British policy now depended very much upon the willingness of the Kuomintang to take the new proposals in good faith, and perhaps to ignore some of the vague promises which Britain was not yet in a position to keep.

The problem of implementation of the Memorandum's provisions drew a clear distinction between the techniques of policy formulation and diplomatic application. The December Memorandum was clearly a

---

[16]Fung, *op. cit.*, p. 103.
[17]Text of a lecture delivered to the Institute of Politics, Williamstown, Mass., in August 1927: Sir Arthur Willert, *Aspects of British Foreign Policy* (New Haven: Institute of Politics; Yale University Press, 1928), pp. 69-70.
[18]Teichman, *op. cit.*, p. 49: Fung, *op. cit.*, p. 103.

document of policy. It outlined broad areas of intent rather than detailing specific measures to be taken to achieve such ends. That particular responsibility lay with the British Legation and the Consular Service, whose experience and abilities equipped them to liaise with various Chinese governments and make manifest the expressions of goodwill which were emanating from the Foreign Office.

In replacing Sir Ronald Macleay with Miles Lampson the British government was clearly intent on paying the Chinese the compliment of sending one of its most skilful and accomplished diplomats. Lampson was no stranger to China: he had been First Secretary in Peking from 1916 to 1920 and had dealt extensively with the question of Shantung when in the British delegation to the Washington Conference.[19] Earlier in his career he had occupied minor positions in the embassy in Tokyo, and although for much of the 1920s his work was done in the Central Department of the Foreign Office, his appointment as Minister to Peking in September 1926 gave due recognition to the *forte* of an able man at the peak of his powers. He had, moreover, gained the reputation within the Far Eastern Department of being Chamberlain's "blue-eyed boy."[20]

There was little doubt that his expertise and insight was sorely needed in Peking. The men 'on the spot' had, it seemed to the Foreign Office, been making unqualified and unauthorised judgments and expressions of value on sensitive issues, thereby threatening whatever credibility remained to Britain in the South. As Pratt acidly minuted: " . . . [the] Legation backed the wrong horse in China . . . [when] they had no right to be backing any horse at all."[21]

On his arrival, Lampson made swift efforts to restore the balance of favour. Instead of making straight for Peking, he made his first call in Hankow, where he extended three days of talks into two weeks of "informal conversations" with Eugene Chen, Minister for Foreign Affairs of the Kuomintang Government and a politician with a noted hostility to Britain.[22] Lampson was, strictly speaking, not making this visit as British Minister, as he had not yet presented his credentials to any Chinese authority. Richard

---

[19]The biographical information on Lampson is taken from David Steeds, "The British Approach to China during the Lampson Period, 1926–1933, with special reference to the Shanghai Incident of 1932" in Ian Nish ed., *Some Foreign Attitudes to Republican China: papers by Taichiro Mitani, David Steeds, Ann Trotter, Dudley Cheke* (London: International Centre for Economics and Related Disciplines, London School of Economics, n.d.), pp. 26-27.
[20]Megginson, *op. cit.*, p. 217: the epithet is attributed to Frank Ashton-Gwatkin. Megginson further notes that Lampson was in agreement with many of Pratt's ideas.
[21]*FO* 371/11661: F5202/10/10: quoted in Stremski, *op. cit.*, p. 101.
[22]Fung, *op. cit.*, pp. 111-12. Stremski notes that Chen begged Lampson to extend his stay in Hankow beyond the three days it had taken them to discuss salient issues, so that the public would not conclude that the talks had been broken off: *op. cit.*, p. 101n.

Stremski indicates that Lampson travelled on his own initiative, as the Kuomintang's November victories in the Yangtze Valley made it imperative that an early channel of communication be established, despite the formal snub this delivered to Peking.[23] The meeting with Chen provided a concrete indication to the Kuomintang that Britain was prepared to do business, without the problems involved in formal recognition of what Britain still regarded as a provincial government.

The value of Lampson's visit was, however, not immediately apparent. The then Minister of Finance of the Peking Government, Wellington Koo, noted in his *Memoir* that it had left a "very unfavourable impression," for the tacit recognition it gave to the Kuomintang was not welcomed by the government of Chang Tso-lin, which the British still recognised as the Chinese government *de facto* pending the establishment of a viable alternative.[24] Moreover, the meetings with Chen were swiftly followed by the forcible occupation of the British concessions at Hankow and Kiukiang. Nationalist forces seemed unwilling to control the riotous mob responsible, and British defenders were unable to repel it by force for fear of a repetition of the May 30th Incident.

The occupations occurred on January 3rd, two days after the formal transfer of the Kuomintang Government from Canton to Wuhan (Hankow), and in the eyes of many British officials clearly demonstrated a premeditated attempt by Bolshevik agitators to provoke a shooting incident or to remove the concession from British control.[25] A formal retrocession of the two concessions was subsequently negotiated by Chen and the First Secretary of the British Legation, Owen O'Malley, and while this agreement purported to settle the issue by placing the administration of the former concession in the hands of a Sino-British joint municipal council, sceptics in the Legation and the British Government were reluctant to give much credence to the safeguards thereby established.[26] While it is possible that the incident may have embarrassed a Kuomintang which was warming to British overtures, the bloodless fall of the Hankow and Kiukiang concessions could neither be excused nor reversed without incurring a severe loss of credibility. The

---

[23]Stremski, *loc. cit.*

[24]V. K. Wellington Koo, *The Wellington Koo Memoir* (New York: Chinese Oral History Project of the East Asian Institute of Columbia University, Part II: Microfilming Corporation of America, 1978), vol. III, p. 121.

[25]Fung, *op. cit.,* p. 115: evidence suggests that the movement was in fact truly spontaneous, causing some embarrassment to the Hankow *regime*.

[26]Fung, *op. cit.*, p. 128: a fuller treatment of the Chen-O'Malley negotiations may be found in Lee En-han, *China's Recovery of the British Hankow and Kiukiang Concessions in 1927* (n.p.: University of Western Australia Centre for Far Eastern Studies, n.d.).

effect of Lampson's promising overture to the South was thus largely negated, with a loss of faith on both sides.

Political opinion in Britain demanded the speedy despatch of troops to protect the International Settlement at Shanghai from a fate similar to that suffered by Hankow. Although Chen and the Legation came to an understanding that the Shanghai Defence Force would be restricted to a purely defensive role, they found themselves further embarrassed by the Nanking Incident of 24 March 1927. In the process of sacking the Chinese City within Nanking, Nationalist troops overran the British, American and Japanese consulates and concessions, wounding the British Consul and killing three other Britons. British and American warships eventually pacified the city by shelling, but the damage done to relations between the Legation and the Kuomintang was considerable. Demands for restitution were evaded or met by counter-demands for restitution for British killings of Chinese citizens, and the issue dragged on until August 1928. Even the more belligerent members of the British Cabinet felt a sense of frustration in their quest for a fitting response to the outrage: Winston Churchill noted that "punishing China is like flogging a jellyfish."[27]

Such public erosions of the status of Britons in China made it increasingly difficult for the Legation to pursue the policy of conciliation of the Kuomintang which the December Memorandum required. Fung characterises the compromise reached as a mixture of "conciliation and firmness":[28] the demands for protection made by the British communities in China could not easily be squared with a desire to reach a *rapprochement* with the party which continued to direct its public energies against the very existence of such communities. The Legation could be forgiven for a certain resentment of the position in which it had been placed by the policymakers at the Foreign Office: even Lampson, a prominent architect of the new policy, was finding its implementation more difficult than its formulation. The Legation was much exasperated by the fact that many of its decisions now depended on the direction taken by the Kuomintang, the orientation of which remained unclear despite the reported purge of Communist and other left-wing elements in April 1927. Wracked by power-struggles throughout the year, the Kuomintang was consistently determined to maintain the initiative *vis-à-vis* Britain, and could not therefore be seen publicly to be following the British lead. Particularly in the autumn of 1927, when the Northern Expedition appeared to be stalled and Chiang Kai-shek, a potential ally, briefly resigned his position as party leader, the policy appeared to have

---

[27]Quoted in Louis, *op. cit.*, p. 133: this also provides the source of detail on the Nanking Incident.
[28]Fung, *op. cit.* ch. 7, *passim.*

been conceived in error. In a lecture to the Imperial Defence College in February 1928, Pratt admitted that he believed that China might continue without a central government "perhaps for a generation or two," and while he appeared sanguine about the prospects for progress in China despite this outlook, it was doubtful that business interests which looked for a swift settlement and the stabilisation of trading conditions shared his optimism.[29] The threat of a permanently cantonised China loomed, and with it the attendant horror of provincial governments taking the December Memorandum revenue grants into their own hands and levying arbitrary tariffs on foreign trade. The main bulwark between the foreign merchant and the provincial authorities had always consisted of the inviolable integrity of the Chinese Maritime Customs Service. Yet by the end of 1927 it appeared that even this institution was on the verge of fragmentation, leaving British trade open to all manner of extortion.

---

[29]"Tendencies and Aspirations in China", a lecture contained in *Pratt Papers* file 66.

# 3
# Synarchy and Revenue

"By giving away shadows, British officials hoped to retain substance."[1] As a critique of the December Memorandum, this provides a fair summary of Foreign Office attitudes towards Britain's stake in the Chinese Maritime Customs Service. The Peking Tariff Conference had assured China that she would regain control over her tariff rates by 1929; but while this promise had been confirmed in the Memorandum, Britain had yet to put forward proposals concerning the eventual return to Chinese control of the agency which administered that tariff on behalf of the Chinese Government. As the Memorandum contained the caveat that suitable concessions would be negotiated only with a government which claimed to speak for the whole of China, the Customs question had not been of immediate significance at the time of the Memorandum's promulgation. As if gratuitously to add to the concerns of the Foreign Office and the Peking Legation, the Peking government dismissed the Inspector-General of Customs, Sir Francis Aglen, in January 1927, thus throwing the question of the future administration of the Customs into serious doubt.

Founded in 1854, the Imperial Maritime Customs Service had as its initial object the safeguarding of the Imperial customs revenue from the ravages of the Taiping Rebellion. Its administration was regularised in 1858 as part of the Treaty of Tientsin, and the British vice-consul at Shanghai, Horatio Nelson Lay, was appointed its first *tsung shui-wu ssu*. The Chinese designation was simply 'Chief Commissioner', but Lay adopted the translation 'Inspector-General of Customs', and the usage stuck.[2] Lay's arrogance in dealing with the Ch'ing, a trait which had proved so effective during his Tientsin negotiations, led in 1865 to his replacement by his

---

[1]Reprinted with permission from *Diplomacy and Enterprise: British China Policy 1933–1937* by Stephen Lyon Endicott (Vancouver: University of British Columbia Press, 1975), p. 9. All rights reserved by the Publisher.
[2]Jonathan Spence, *To Change China: Western Advisors in China 1620–1960* (New York: Penguin, 1980), p. 102.

deputy Robert Hart, who had initially been seconded from the Consular Service to replace Lay while the latter took two years' leave.

Hart's approach to the position was diametrically opposed to Lay's. While his predecessor was renowned for his refusal to submit to "Asiatic barbarians," Hart took cognisance of the realities of his situation and proceeded to build an administration which had as its object the service of the Chinese interest.[3] It is not the intention here to detail the remarkable career of Hart in this post, but it will suffice to say that he was universally recognised as the "Great I.-G.," a legendary figure respected by foreigners and Chinese alike.[4] Although his methods were often autocratic and his manner at times difficult, there was no doubting the remarkable sense of responsibility with which he carried out his duties to the Imperial Government and to China. Hart survived the siege of the Legations in 1900, and it is illuminating to note that immediately afterwards he set himself to writing a sympathetic exposition of the Chinese mind and character.[5]

Hart retired from the Service in 1907 and died in 1911. He could therefore not fairly be held responsible for the fall of the Ch'ing, nor was he obliged to express his opinions on the future of the Republic or the rise of Chinese nationalism. One suspects that such political utterances might have served to tarnish a spotless reputation, the lustre of which could only be brightened by comparison with the compromises future Inspectors-General were to make in what they held to be China's best interests. Hart left express instructions that his diaries were not to be published.[6] No such stipulations were applied to his voluminous Semi-Official correspondence, much of which gives insights into the apparently miraculous manner by which he had managed to transform the Customs into an international, non-partisan bureaucratic institution which provided the greatest single source of secure revenue for the Ch'ing. By effectively combining Western expertise and Chinese objectives, Hart had created an excellent institutional example of

---

[3] Pratt's assessment of Lay's character is encapsulated in a quotation he cites: "I need scarcely observe that the notion of a gentleman acting under an Asiatic barbarian is preposterous." FO 371/13905/37: F 911/52/10.

[4] Hart's career is documented in exhaustive detail in Stanley F. Wright, *Hart and the Chinese Customs* (Belfast: Wm. Mullan and Son, 1950). A more impressionistic account is to be found in Spence, *op. cit.*, ch. 4, while the immense collection of letters Hart addressed to the Customs' Non-Resident Secretary in London, J.D. Campbell, are published in *The I.G. in Peking: Letters of Robert Hart, Chinese Maritime Customs 1868–1907* eds. John King Fairbank, Katherine Frost Bruner, Elizabeth MacLeod Matheson, 2 vols (Cambridge, Mass.: The Belknap Press of Harvard University Press, 1975).

[5] Published as *These from the Land of Sinim* (London, 1901).

[6] Correspondence about the Hart diaries was conducted between Frederick Maze, Commissioner of Customs at Tientsin, and the journalist J.O.P. Bland in 1923 and 1924: see *MP* Ia/XIX, pp. 19-23.

what Fairbank has termed 'synarchy'; that is to say, a true partnership between Chinese and foreign personnel, where the foreigners benefitted China and foreign traders alike by acting as "intermediaries between East and West."[7] His achievement was recognised by the most exalted form of commemoration Shanghai society could confer: an imposing statue on the Bund.[8]

Hart had maintained a service, the function of which was to assess the duty to be paid on all maritime imports and exports through China's treaty ports. Since 1842 this rate had been set at five per cent on the value *(ad valorem)* of both imported and exported goods, although the actual tariffs would fluctuate in order to maintain these levels of import revenue or to encourage exports. Revenue also accrued to the Customs through the collection of coast trade duty and transit dues, while other income from tonnage dues and famine relief surtaxes was retained in separate accounts.[9] In addition, the Customs Service administered the assessment of Native Customs revenue within a fifty-*li* radius of the treaty ports, but under Hart's regime the foreign Commissioners of Customs at each port were never to deal with the receipts which such assessments yielded. This was the responsibility of the Superintendent of Customs, a Chinese appointee equal in status to the Commissioner and answerable to Peking for the correct remission of revenue to the Imperial Treasury. The large and talented foreign staff establishment which Hart created thus had the function of administering Customs affairs at each port, ensuring that the correct assessments of duty were made and that neither the Empire nor its foreign traders had cause to complain of any malpractice.

The establishment of an impartial, efficient and profitable buffer had a corresponding effect on the stability of the Customs revenue. Thus when the Treaty of Shimonoseiki, which followed the Sino-Japanese War of 1895, placed an impossibly large indemnity on the Imperial Treasury, the Customs revenue was used as security and principal for the floating of internal and foreign loans, the better to settle the debt.[10] While the Boxer Indemnity

---

[7]John King Fairbank, "Synarchy inder the Treaties", in Fairbank ed. *Chinese Thought and Institutions* (Chicago, Ill.: The University of Chicago Press, 1957), pp. 204-31, esp. pp. 222-23.

[8]"The Great I.G.", editorial in *NCH* (17 December 1927) commemorating the removal of Hart's statue to a site outside the new Shanghai Customs House.

[9]Stanley F. Wright, *The Collection and Disposal of the Maritime and Native Customs Revenue since the Revolution of 1911, with an Account of the Loan Services administered by the Inspector General of Customs* 2nd. ed. (Shanghai: Statistical Department of the Inspectorate General of Customs, 1927), pp. 24-5.

[10] Between 1895 and 1898 the Imperial Government contracted foreign loans totalling 53 million pounds sterling (equivalent to 260 million dollars): by 1925 the repayments on the

imposed in 1901 was to be repaid by revenue raised by the Native Customs, in practice a substantial amount of Maritime Customs revenue was required to supplement payments from this source.[11] Although managed by Hart and secured in great measure by his reputation, the foreign loan issues were projects of the Imperial Treasury, which had full control over Customs receipts. Hart's probity and influence, however, ensured that the Treasury honoured its obligations to the international financial community.

The revolution of 1911 fundamentally altered the Chinese fiscal landscape. It could no longer be guaranteed that Superintendents of Customs at outlying ports would interpret their duty to China as an obligation to remit revenue directly to the Republican government. This was a situation as dangerous to the interests of foreign states and individuals who held bonds secured on the revenue as it was to the finances of the fledgling Republic. By order of the Inspector-General, therefore, the revenue collected at each port was collected by the foreign Commissioner, who deposited it in one of the three foreign banks with the greatest stake in foreign loan obligations for credit to the account of the Inspector-General in Shanghai.[12] The Diplomatic Body subsequently negotiated with the Inspector-General to establish a machinery for the appropriation of revenue to the service of foreign obligations. This resulted in the Custodian Bank Agreement of 1912, whereby the managers of the three custodian banks formed a commission for the apportionment of customs receipts in order of their initial hypothecation.[13] While the safeguards thus implemented protected the credit of China, they also bound her most constant source of revenue far more closely to the interests of foreign powers. Whereas before 1907 the reputation and force of personality of Sir Robert Hart had been enough to convince creditors of the security of the Customs Revenue, the Custodian Bank Agreement placed the onus on successive republican governments to convince the Diplomatic Body, as the trustee of the revenue in the name of foreign bondholders, that they were eligible for the disbursement of revenue. The fact that the Inspector-General's recognition of a government generally

---

outstanding portions of these loans still amounted to over 2½ million pounds (12 million dollars). Wright, *op. cit.*, pp. 59, 213.

[11] The sum total of principal and interest which the Boxer Indemnity imposed on the Imperial Treasury amounted to 982,238,150 Haikwan taels, (equivalent to $707,211,468 at the prevalent rate of exchange) although by 1926 much of the outstanding debt had been renegotiated into funds for the benefit of the Chinese nation. Wright, *loc.cit.*

[12] The approved banks were the Russo-Asiatic Bank, the Deutsch-Asiatische Bank and the Hongkong and Shanghai Banking Corporation. In 1917 China declared war on Germany, and the Deutsch-Asiatisch Bank was deleted from the Custodian Bank Agreement, while in 1924 the Russo-Asiatic Bank went into voluntary liquidation. This left the Hongkong and Shanghai Banking Corporation as the sole custodian of revenue hypothecated for loan repayment.

[13] Wright, *op. cit.*, pp. 3-7.

accompanied that of the Diplomatic Body in Peking had two complementary effects: it required any faction seeking the keys to the national treasury to take and hold Peking while setting up some semblance of constitutional government acceptable to the Powers; and it gave those Powers far greater control in the internal politics of the Chinese Republic. Henceforth China was to be made increasingly aware of her obligations to foreign bondholders.[14]

It is fair to say that Francis Aglen was genuinely concerned for the fate of China, as he perceived it. It is nevertheless true that his position as *de facto* arbiter of the destiny of Customs revenue had placed him in a situation which might have entrapped even his predecessor. Aglen was increasingly aware of the insult to Chinese nationalism which the continued existence of the Custodian Bank Agreement represented. He nevertheless found it necessary to maintain the integrity of the Service increasingly by the force of his own personality. Thus the issue of foreign control of the Customs was raised in a manner which Hart had never had to countenance. Aglen was as committed as he could be to carrying on Hartian principles in what he considered the best traditions of the Service. The two men had built up a fine rapport over the three years in which Aglen had been informally designated Hart's successor, and the former, by virtue of his position, certainly had the right to invoke the protection of Hart's mantle.[15]

Aglen was, however, of the belief that China was entering a state of great flux, and that the Customs was as liable to change in its role as any other Chinese institution. His views on the prospects for Chinese nationalism and the eventual sinification of the service were moderately liberal, and he was certainly no advocate of the indiscriminate growth of foreign tutelage over the Chinese. He was rather fond of the imagery of "the good old Customs ship," with himself at the helm, steering through the uncharted and inhospitable waters of Chinese factionalism in the hope that a safe haven

---

[14]The Customs revenue was in fact apportioned according to strict priorities. The first charge on the revenue was the administration of a full-strength Service, and the banking costs which such administration entailed. Next in line came appropriations to special projects for the service of China which the Diplomatic Body had approved. Then money would be appropriated for special Service expenses, such as the acquisition of land for new customs houses or the compensation of customs officers robbed or wounded in the pursuit of their duties. Only then could the remaining revenue be applied to the service of foreign loans, any surplus being swept into the Boxer Indemnity fund. Other revenues, such as tonnage dues, were also appropriated for special purposes, in that particular case the maintenance of harbour safety. Wright, *op. cit.*, pp. 24-5.

[15]The succession to Hart had nevertheless caused problems. See below, p. 70n.

would eventually be found.[16] This attitude was expressed in more literal terms in a letter to the London Non-Resident Secretary in 1922:

> It seems to me that the service has gone through two stages and is on the verge of a third. At first we were a fine Chinese institution maintained and supported by the Govt. because we supplied a certain income which the Govt. found very useful. Then the loans came and we became a foreign interest with the Chinese Govts. interest still predominant. The [Boxer] Indemnity gave the foreign Governments a financial interest in us; the Revolution which gave us control of the revenue and loans service, transformed us into an unofficial foreign "caisse de la dette", a position full of anomalies but on the whole suitable to the times. Awkward questions were kept in abeyance and China's credit abroad was maintained, while the shadow of China managing her own affairs without foreign interference was preserved. The last stage in this development has been reached owing to the virtual cessation of central govt. authority and the necessity of carrying on administration with borrowed money. The Customs is now an imperium in imperio practically independent in matters of government finance but in the last resort resting not on the Chinese Govt. but on the foreign powers. The position is becoming more difficult and must undergo modification one way or the other during the next three years.[17]

Aglen guarded against burdening the revenue with further foreign obligations, and looked somewhat askance at the attempts of the Powers to intervene in China's reconstruction effort. In 1918, for example, the Diplomatic Body had unilaterally extended its trusteeship beyond that of the Customs revenue hypothecated to the service of foreign loans: once the revenue began to show a surplus, that too was annexed to purposes which the Body decided worthwhile, such as the support of Chinese legations abroad and the development of a modern educational system.[18] Although Aglen was aware of the need to maintain "China's credit abroad" in order to secure the funds required for reconstruction, he increasingly opposed the attempts of the China Consortium to raise foreign loans on the Customs

---

[16]For Aglen's metaphor, see FO 228/3740/5A/68A 1928: Edwardes letter to Lampson of 21 February 1928.

[17]*Aglen Papers*: Inspector-General's Correspondence: Aglen letter to Acheson of 28 February 1922.

[18]Andrew J. Nathan, *Peking Politics 1918–1923: Factionalism and the Failure of Constitutionalism* (Berkeley, Calif.: University of California Press, 1976), pp. 79-80.

revenue, a practice which tended to undercut the stability of the Chinese financial markets.[19]

In seeking to bolster the domestic loan market to defend against foreign intervention, Aglen was undertaking one of the most controversial moves of his career. Dayer and McElderry have demonstrated how foreign banking interests had effectively turned the Shansi *ch'ien-chuang* native banks into comprador institutions by the simple device of alowing them to resell foreign bond issues at higher prices.[20] Until the establishment of the Bank of China and the Bank of Communications in 1911, foreign banks had the monopoly on loan issue trading and provided the only outlet for foreign exchange. The modernisation of the Chinese banking industry, pioneered by figures such as Chang Kia-ngau, was thus as much a nationalistic endeavour as anything else.[21] Aglen's contribution to this enterprise consisted of the arrangement and underwriting of a Consolidated Loan Fund in 1921. This 'sinking fund' amalgamated a proportion of the surpluses of the Customs, Salt, Wine and Tobacco collectorates into a source of security for domestic bond issues, the security ultimately to be guaranteed by Aglen in his capacity as Inspector-General.[22]

The immediate effect of the Consolidated Fund was to save the Peking government of the day from bankruptcy: its credit with foreign banks had all but expired and there had been fears that the Japanese government would intervene to secure payments of its Nishihara loans, contracted in 1905.[23] In the longer term, the Fund saved the Customs revenues from the threat of direct hypothecation by the Diplomatic Body, thereby relieving the pressure on the Peking Government to satisfy unreasonable foreign demands. It created an alternative form of security for the Customs Service itself in the form of interested Chinese bondholders, and gave the modern Chinese banks a greater stake in the reconstruction campaign. However, it also created the potential for future disaster. The appropriation of part of the surplus Customs revenue in the support of loan services threatened to drain away the healthy surpluses which the Customs was beginning to show, and raised the question of whether, in the event of a crisis, it would be the

---

[19] A fuller treatment of this issue is to be found in Dayer, *Bankers and Diplomats*, ch. 3.

[20] Dayer, *op. cit.*, p. 7: Andrea Lee Mc Elderry, *Shanghai Old-Style Banks (ch'ien-chuang) 1800–1935: A Traditional Institution in a Changing Society* (Ann Arbor, Mich.: Center for Chinese Studies, The University of Michigan, 1976), pp. 17-21.

[21] Dayer, *op. cit.*, pp. 85-6. Chang was appointed assistant general manager of the Bank of China in Peking in 1917, and forged close links with Aglen. *BDRC*, vol. I pp. 26-29.

[22] Nathan, *op. cit.*, pp. 88-89n: Wright, *Collection and Disposal*, pp. 190-92. Annual hypothecations to the Consolidated Loan Fund from the various revenue surpluses totalled 24 million U.S. dollars, to service annual principal and interest repayments which in 1925 amounted to 25,167,920 dollars (Wright, *op. cit.*, pp. 236-37).

[23] See above, p. 17.

Chinese or the foreign creditors who would be given priority in repayment schedules. The personal intervention by Aglen in moving against foreign control, while lauded by Dayer, also had the effect of making him the arbiter of Chinese finances and linked the Inspectorate-General to the emergent banking clique in Peking of which Chang's Chinese Bankers' Association was the driving force.

It was with some justice that Aglen could claim to have taken steps to extract the Customs Service from the unpleasant situation in which the Custodian Bank Agreement had placed it. However, he had created a role for himself which was nothing if not political. From the Olympian heights of his self-styled impartiality he would look down upon the Chinese scene and give magisterial judgments on the viability and rectitude of each of the warring factions. He shared with Macleay a prudent admiration for Wu P'ei-fu as the general most likely to prevail in the civil war, and a distaste for the politics of Canton in general and of Sun Yat-sen in particular.[24] His personal involvement in the internal affairs of Peking governments had earned him the epithet of "super-minister of finance," while his close association with the banking circles in the capital drew increasing attention to the pivotal nature of his role.[25] His creation of the Consolidated Loan Fund had been made against the express wishes of the Diplomatic Body, which believed that the distribution of surpluses was the exclusive preserve of Chinese governments.[26] Moreover, in funnelling the Customs surplus into those projects of fiscal reconstruction he believed worthwhile, Aglen unwisely neglected the claims of the Cantonese. His view of the integrity and impartiality of the Service, though possibly correct in the short term, was to create resentments and prejudices which would endanger that impartiality sooner than he thought possible.

The only exception made to the allocation by the Diplomatic Body of Customs revenue to the government recognised at Peking had been in 1919 and 1920, the first years when the Customs had reported surplus revenue after the servicing of all loan obligations. The Canton government had made an effective case for a *pro rata* distribution of surplus Customs receipts, and

---

[24]In April 1922 Aglen had written to Acheson "What is wanted for the moment is of course a Dictator but Wu Pei Fu will not assume this role openly," while in October 1924 he wrote to Bowra "If Wu comes through he will be in a position of enormous prestige and power with practically all China at his feet, and I think he will make short work of Sun Wen [Sun Yat-sen] and his Bolshevik crowd at Canton." *AP*, Inspector-General's Correspondence, letters of 22 April 1922 and 22 October 1924.

[25]The pejorative use of the term "super-minister of finance" appears in *Koo Memoir*, vol. III p. 129 *inter alia*. In this instance it refers to the close connection between Aglen, Chang Kia-ngau and other members of the Peking banking clique, such as Li Ming. Such connections effectively tied the hands of any Peking Minister of Finance.

[26]Wright, *Collection and Disposal*, p. 190.

successfully claimed 13.7 per cent of the surplus, a percentage representing the proportion of Chinese territory it controlled. Factional fighting in early 1920, however, led to an unseemly quarrel within the Canton regime as to which faction within the government was entitled to receive the funds. In May the appropriated funds were reserved in a special bank account in Shanghai, where they accumulated until December. By that time the Diplomatic Body had been convinced of the apparent folly of "giving these subsidies to an officially unrecognised government out of funds which technically belonged to the Central Government," and discontinued the practice, reserving the disputed amount for the upkeep of central government institutions. Moreover, almost all the Customs surplus was to be appropriated to the Consolidated Loan Fund as of March 1921.[27]

The Canton government returned to its claims with renewed vigour in June 1923. No longer willing to count on the benevolence of the Diplomatic Body or of the Inspector-General, it backed up its demands with a threat to take control of the Customs administration in the city. The threat this posed to the integrity of the Customs, and, more to the point, the continued collection of revenue to secure loans and maintain the Consolidated Fund, led the Powers to conduct a naval demonstration in the harbour of Canton in December.[28] The warning this provided served to humiliate Sun Yat-sen, whom Aglen reported to be "in a desperate situation" by March 1924.[29] The provocative character of the warning had removed the immediate threat to the Customs, but had only served to exacerbate the hostility which had developed in the nationalist movement towards what it saw as the immoral foreign control over Chinese funds. There is little doubt that the demonstration of foreign force in defence of foreign interests provided a graphic illustration to the text of anti-imperialist revolution which the Soviet agitator Borodin had begun to preach, and served as a profound disillusionment to those nationalists who had viewed the Washington treaties as evidence of the Powers' sympathy towards their ideals and aspirations.[30]

In his refusal to concede ground to the political manifestations of Chinese nationalism Aglen stood shoulder-to-shoulder with the Legation and the rest of the Diplomatic Body. While he may have been motivated by a

---

[27] A detailed account of this episode may be found in Wright, op. cit., pp. 164-67. In 1925 the reported Customs surplus amounted to 18,365,830 Haikwan taels, (equivalent to \$15,427,297) of which 18,014,670 (\$15,132,322) were allocated to the Consolidated Loan Fund. (*Ibid.*, p. 213.)

[28] Dayer, op. cit. , pp. 163-65.

[29] AP, Inspector-General's Correspondence: letter from Aglen to Bowra of 11 March 1924.

[30] P. Cavendish, "Anti-Imperialism in the Kuomintang, 1923–8" in Jerome Ch'en and Nicholas Tarling eds., *Studies in the Social History of China and South-East Asia: Essays in Memory of Victor Purcell* (Cambridge: Cambridge University Press, 1970), pp. 26-27.

determination to ensure the integrity of the Customs and the revenue, he appeared to many foreigners and Chinese as nothing more than a fiscal autocrat who was acting in concert with the Powers. His continued support for Chinese fiscal autonomy in the face of continued Consortium pressure had not resonated at all in the South, although it had led the Foreign Office to search for a new policy on Chinese finances.[31] Aglen viewed the eruption of the nationalist movement in 1925 with awe and fear: "the people of China are beginning to mutter and sooner or later there will be an explosion and the authorities, or the so-called authorities, military and civil, will endeavour to turn popular discontent against the foreigner as they have done in the past." Writing in 1926 he stated that "the Chinese Revolution has not yet taken place. 1911 was only a pseudo-Revolution–a movement to get rid of one set of corrupt rulers to make way for a worse set. The real Revolution, when it comes, will be a Revolution of the people of China and it will be one which will make the world sit up and take notice."[32]

These prophecies of doom notwithstanding, there is little indication that after 1925 Aglen really endeavoured to come to terms with the nationalist movement or to comprehend its real force. Although still at the helm of the Customs, he had found himself increasingly blown off course. It had been his intention to retire in 1925 at the age of sixty, and not to create an aura of indispensability around himself as he believed Hart had: "private interests and inclinations are drawing me home and I am only staying here because public interests make it impossible for me to cut the knot without a certain degree of friction."[33]

Dayer claims that Aglen had become so obstructive to British plans for the reorganisation of Chinese finances that the Foreign Office colluded in his eventual dismissal.[34] The evidence for such collusion is scanty at best, and the nature of Aglen's relationship with Whitehall indicates that such an assertion is improbable. Although Aglen had made little secret of his distaste for some Foreign Office policies, attributing their genesis to the opinions of those men, such as Sir John Jordan and Sir Charles Addis, whom he regarded as out of touch with Chinese affairs, in fact he endeavoured to maintain channels of communication with the Far Eastern Department, with the aim of keeping it informed of his policy and explaining the reasoning behind it. The Non-Resident Secretary in London was frequently authorised to give informal briefings to Foreign Office officials, especially during November and December of 1926 when Aglen foresaw a real threat to the

---

[31]Dayer, *op. cit.*, pp. 201-04.
[32]*AP*, Inspector-General's Correspondence: letters from Aglen to Bowra of 11 December 1925 and 29 January 1926.
[33]*AP*, Inspector-General's Correspondence: letter from Aglen to Bowra of 17 May 1926.
[34]Dayer, *op. cit.*, pp. 209, 216n.

integrity of the Customs from Kuomintang victories on the Yangtze and feared that the Powers would be unable to muster sufficient unity or resolve to defend the administration from the wrath of the Nationalists.[35] However, the Inspector-General was astute enough to determine that direct reliance on British support would threaten his position and the perceived integrity of the Customs.

> My position does not depend so much now on the power and prestige of the British Government. If it depended solely on that I am afraid it would be a very poor outlook because British prestige has never been at such a low ebb in China. Ultimately, of course, everything depends on my extraterritorialised status, and if Great Britain gives that up I could not hold my post and should not attempt to do so. In the last resort, however, it is not the British Government's power and prestige which will keep me in office but the general feeling of the Chinese whose interests are concentrated in the Customs that it would be undesirable to have too drastic a change.[36]

Aglen's loan policies had drawn almost constant criticism from the Foreign Office, though in the main his position had been supported by the Peking Legation. Objections to Aglen's actions at first stemmed from their independence and apparent disregard for the interests of foreign bondholders which they indicated. After the shift in Foreign Office policy, however, Aglen was criticised for a heavy reliance upon Peking politicians and financiers, and for his disdain for the emergence of the South. Increasing evidence of loans made to warlords on the security of the Consolidated Fund tended to worry the Foreign Office, which was concerned not only that Britain might be tainted by implication, but also that such loans might be used for military purposes, despite Aglen's assurances to the contrary. If those military purposes happened to be for the checking of the Northern Expedition, then the Foreign Office had every right to be alarmed, as it was possible that Aglen's loans to the North would obliterate any advances Britain had managed to make south of the Yangtze.

The Foreign Office could not dispatch Aglen: neither could he utterly repudiate its support. There was little love lost between the two nonetheless. Referring to the recent change in personnel at the Far Eastern Department, Aglen confided in Bowra:

> I hope Wright has been very careful in what he has said to Pratt and Mounsey. I know nothing about the latter but I seriously distrust the

---

[35]Copies of Inspector-General's telegrams from Peking to London are in *MP* Ia/II, pp. 6-21.
[36]*AP*, Inspector-General's Correspondence: letter from Aglen to Bowra of 26 May 1926.

former. I am kept pretty well posted by the Legation in all they receive from the Foreign Office, and I think that the advice they have been getting from a so-called expert is highly dangerous . . . I seriously distrust the gentlemen who are now running China policy at your end.[37]

Pratt could be equally scathing about the expert attention Aglen had given to the Chinese political scene: he was later to compare Aglen's attitude to that of Horatio Lay.[38] Having spent a great deal of time in countering the effects of Aglen's obstinacy and his inflated view of his role in Chinese affairs, Pratt must have hoped that British control over the Customs could be maintained without such gratuitous attempts to court disaster and jeopardise its safety.

In December 1926 Aglen was informed by the Peking Shui-wu Ch'u that he was to begin to collect revenue from the Customs surtaxes of 2½ per cent which the Washington Conference powers had in principle granted in 1921.[39] In a cable to Lampson, Aglen warned him that this collection would have to proceed slowly in the South to maintain the integrity of the Customs, as the Nationalists had threatened to "smash the existing administration" if the surtaxes were to be collected.[40] Aglen himself had proceeded south in January 1927 in order to "discuss Customs affairs with the [Shanghai] Commissioner and Bankers."[41] In fact his mission was to discuss the surtax situation with Eugene Chen at Hankow. This may have represented the first time he seriously considered the implications for the Customs of a successful Nationalist drive north. Chen had evidently been disturbed by the proposal to collect surtaxes in the South to fund the Northern war effort, particularly as Shanghai remained under Northern control.[42] Aglen had, however, received a guarantee from "[an] influential Banker in touch with [the] Nationalist Authorities" to the effect that the Nationalists would not repudiate domestic loans secured on the Customs.[43] Aglen's assessment of

[37]*AP*, Inspector-General's Correspondence: letter from Aglen to Bowra of 7 June 1926. "Wright" was Stanley F. Wright, Aglen's personal secretary, who was in London in part to discuss his recently-published compendium of revenue allocations and loan service transactions, *q.v.* Aglen had previously warned: "[The book] is really a very wonderful piece of work and reflects the greatest credit on him, but it was a description of my doings and whatever he says he must be careful not to speak beyond the book." *Ibid.*, letter from Aglen to Bowra, 17th May 1926.

[38]FO 371/13905/37: F 911/52/10: Pratt minute of 21 February 1929.

[39]*MP* Ia/II p. 20: cable from Aglen to Stephenson, 13 December 1926.

[40]FO 228/3298/200/96 1927: cable from Aglen to Lampson, 22 January 1927.

[41]*NCH*, 8 January 1927, p. 6.

[42]*MP* Ia/II p. 21: cable from Aglen to Stephenson 29 December 1926.

[43]*Ibid.* One assumes that this figure is Chang Kia-ngau, whose role as Peking manager of the Bank of China would place his finger on the political pulse of the South through his

the situation was that the Peking government of Chang Tso-lin would not dare to implement the surtaxes without his approval, which would not be forthcoming given the opposition of the South to the plan.[44] Yet Aglen was summarily dismissed on January 31st even before his return from Hankow for reasons which the Minister of Finance, Wellington Koo, summarised as "insubordination."[45]

The mandate of dismissal caused consternation in diplomatic and financial circles. In an editorial on February 2nd entitled "Financial Suicide", the *North-China Daily News* predicted the ruin of the Customs and the collapse of the value of Chinese securities. It therefore invoked the power of the Diplomatic Body to come to the aid of Customs integrity in the interests of foreign bondholders. The predicted consequence of a Chinese government being able to dismiss the Inspector-General of Customs was for the Customs to pass under Chinese control, "thereby ceasing at once to be adequate security for anything."[46] A deputation of Chinese bankers led by Chang Kia-ngau urged Koo to reconsider the decision in the light of its effect on the financial market, challenging the government either to produce a plan to stabilise the market or to resign.[47] They cited a "loss of confidence" on the part of bondholders reacting to Aglen's removal—a reflection, no doubt, of concern over the succession.

The British Legation was no less concerned, and feared a Chinese Inspector-General swept in on a high tide of nationalist sentiment. In assessing the situation, Lampson informed Chamberlain that:

> We must always remember that the way things have gone in China there is no limit at which the Chinese will stop in their present mood. And in that respect the Northerner is precisely the same animal as the Southerner, though up to date, to give him his due, he has at least preserved the forms of international courtesy in his dealings with foreigners.[48]

---

communications with Head Office in Shanghai. His close association with Aglen also makes him a likely candidate, although other figures in the Peking bankers' clique, such as Li Ming of the Chekiang Industrial Bank, cannot be ruled out.

[44] FO 228/3298/200/94A 1927: Lampson despatch to Chamberlain of 4 February summarising the events of Aglen's dismissal.

[45] *Koo Memoir*, vol. III, p. 130. Although Koo's recollection of the issue which prompted the dismissal was Aglen's refusal to agree to raising a loan on the security of the defunct Austrian indemnity, the facts of Aglen's refusal and the subsequent Diplomatic Body protests remain the same.

[46] *NCH*, 5 February 1927, pp. 186-87.

[47] *Koo Memoir*, vol. III, p. 124: he reports having shrugged off the challenge.

[48] FO 228/3298/200/94A 1927: Lampson despatch to Chamberlain of 4 February.

Lampson had been informed of the proposed dismissal on January 28th and had worked vigorously behind the scenes to save Aglen. He proposed a protest to the Peking Government which would take as its themes the British administrative interest in the Customs "built up over half a century," the need for an efficient Customs administration in British hands, and a British responsibility for the interests of bondholders.[49] None of this made an impression on Koo, who peremptorily dismissed a deputation from the Diplomatic Body without deigning to enter into the details of the case.[50] The most that Lampson could achieve was that as a face-saving measure Aglen was granted a year's leave, to be followed by an involuntary resignation.[51] Lampson regarded this as the best course under the circumstances: "I did carefully consider every means of pressure available to me to insist on seeing a wrong to a British subject put right: but everything seemed to be in the nature of cutting off one's nose to spite one's face."[52] Instead of relying on British "table-thumping," Lampson had taken care to orchestrate pressure from the entire Diplomatic Body. This did not, however, preclude his railing at Wang Ch'ung-hui, the Chief Justice, who had been sent by Koo to negotiate British approval of a successor:

> . . . I spoke very strongly of the contemptible way in which Sir F. Aglen had been treated; he, a man of over thirty years dedicated service to China—17 of them in the immensely responsible position of Inspector-General of Customs—had been dismissed without so much as a hearing. He had been treated worse than a dog, and it was a lesson to all foreigners of the gross ingratitude and lack of all decent feeling on the part of the Chinese nowadays.[53]

In 1898 Britain had exchanged diplomatic notes with the Tsungli Yamen, bringing into effect an agreement that the Inspector-General of Customs would be a British subject for as long as British trade were to be predominant in China. To many Western and Chinese observers it was patently obvious that Japanese and United States trade had by 1927 surpassed that of Britain: however, to appoint a Japanese Inspector-General in the present Chinese political climate would have been considered a gross and dangerous insult. Moreover, there were no Japanese candidates in

---

[49]FO 228/3298/200/80 1927: Lampson cable to Foreign Office of 30 January.

[50]*Koo Memoir*, vol. III, pp. 130-31.

[51]FO 228/3928/200/103 1927: Lampson telegram to Foreign Office of 7 February recording Diplomatic Body meeting with Wai-chiao Pu.

[52]*Ibid.* Privately, however, Lampson recognised that "the fault was partly Aglen's own, for he refused to come back when both Edwardes and I pressed him to." *KD*, f. 53v (1927): February 25, 1927.

[53]FO 228/3298/200/119 1927: Lampson cable to Foreign Office of 15 February 1927.

suitably advanced positions in the Service, with the exception of some commissioners in Manchurian outports. The tenor of comments upon their performance indicated that further promotions were unlikely to be made until Japanese threats to the region subsided.[54] Nevertheless the Japanese Government was particularly concerned about increasing the proportion of their nationals in the Service, and had as early as 1921 made strong representations to this effect.[55] Such factors complicated the diplomacy required to secure a British Inspector-General, although the Tsungli Yamen note appeared not to burden Lampson's conscience. There was no apparent doubt that Aglen's successor would be British.

Indeed, upon Aglen's dismissal the Peking Government had appointed A.H.F. Edwardes, the Chief Secretary of Customs, to the post of Officiating Inspector-General. Edwardes had been Aglen's *de facto* deputy in Peking and had been groomed by him with a view to this eventual promotion.[56] While Lampson was enthusiastic about Edwardes' character and fitness, he was reluctant to endorse him until it was clear that Aglen could not be reinstated. Intelligence from Hankow also indicated that the South was likely to block any attempt by the North to make Customs appointments for the whole of China. The Commissioner of Customs at Hankow, J.W.H. Ferguson, reported that the Nationalists would not recognise any appointments made by Peking and that if Aglen was not reinstated the Service would be disrupted.[57] It seems that only a direct and personal plea from Aglen himself prevented the South from making good on a threat to appoint a separate Inspector-General.[58] However, the spectre of a split administration was never effectively dispelled. As it was, the compromise reached over Aglen's retirement involved the redesignation of Edwardes as Acting Inspector-General (*tai-li tsung shui-wu ssu*) until such time as Aglen should formally leave the Service.[59] This compromise

---

[54]In response to an enquiry as to whether the Commisioner of Customs at Dairen, H. Kishimoto, might be promoted higher, Oswald White, the consul at Dairen, wrote that "I have good reason to believe that in questions which have arisen between the Chinese customs in Dairen and the Kwantung Government, Mr. Kishimoto, in spite of his Japanese ancestry, has shown himself an entirely loyal servant of the Chinese Customs." FO 228/3298/200/125 1927: despatch from White to Sir John Tilley (Ambassador to Tokyo) of 14 February 1927: copy to Peking.

[55]Teichman and Newton at the Legation recalled such Japanese proposals being made to the Washington Conference. FO 228/3590/5A/10 1927: file note of 27 September 1927.

[56]FO 228/3298/200/83 1927: Lampson telegram to F.O. of 31 January 1927.

[57]FO 228/3298/200/117 1927: Ferguson telegram to Edwardes, 14 February 1927, forwarded to Lampson.

[58]FO 228/3298/200/119 1927: Lampson telegram to F.O., 15 February 1927.

[59]FO 228/3928/200/110 1927: Aglen letter to Chen via Ferguson, 10 February 1927.

appeared to mollify Hankow while leaving the confirmation of Edwardes to be settled at a later date.

Wellington Koo recalled that Lampson was initially opposed to Edwardes' appointment and advised him against taking it up.[60] This was an attempt by Lampson to salvage what he could of the situation: with no formal authority over the process, he could at least prevent the consummation of the *fait accompli* by obstructing the appointment of a successor. Wang Ch'ung-hui's informal talks with the Minister, described by the latter as "things . . . developing in a typically Chinese way," were intended to remove the obstruction he was causing.[61] Wang threatened Lampson with the appointment of the man "next to Sir Francis in seniority," the Commissioner of Customs at Shanghai, F. W. Maze. This threat was not reported by Lampson, either because Maze was not taken seriously as a candidate, or as Koo suggests, he was too "independent."[62] The Legation was galvanised into action nevertheless. Writing in 1929, with a great deal of hindsight, the Foreign Office official George Mounsey noted that "the ex-I.G. . . . had specially selected and trained Mr. Edwardes for the post with the express idea it now appears of keeping Mr. Maze out."[63] Edwardes was, for better or for worse, the choice of the Peking establishment, and as such received this ringing endorsement from Lampson:

> . . . from what I have seen of [Edwardes] since my arrival he appears to be a man of tact and of sane and balanced judgment fully qualified to undertake the very responsible and delicate duties with which he finds himself so unexpectedly charged. In addition to his other qualifications, he has a sense of humour; and in all seriousness I consider that almost essential in existing conditions in the country: it may very well save Mr. Edwardes' sanity and health. Mr. Edwardes has the advantage of being comparitively young. If all goes well, his appointment should thus secure to us the Inspector-Generalship for many years to come, and that is in itself a great thing.[64]

Lampson had, moreover, negotiated the support of the Japanese Minister for a British appointment, using the rhetoric of security and stability to override any claims to the succession Yoshizawa might have entertained.[65]

---

[60]*Koo Memoir*, vol. III, pp. 131-34.
[61]FO 228/3298/200/105 1927: minute on visit of Wang Ch'ung-hui, 9 January 1927.
[62]*Koo Memoir*, vol. III, pp. 133-34.
[63]FO 371/13905: F284/52/10: Mounsey minute of 17 January 1929.
[64]FO 228/3298/200/121 1927: Lampson despatch of 15 February 1927.
[65]*Ibid.*: it appears, however, that the promises of Japanese support were in fact more conditional than Lampson had initially appreciated. See below, p. 63.

It was indeed fortunate that Lampson had a ready-made and willing successor to Aglen on hand, particularly one as well-groomed for the position as Edwardes. Despite the difficulties which the Foreign Office had had with Aglen in the past, it was considered an immeasurable safeguard to British trade to have a British Inspector-General in charge of the Customs. The service claimed impartiality and internationality, and in many ways fully lived up to its claims: nevertheless, it had a predominantly British composition and as such found itself subject to peculiarly British biases. In practice Hart's doctrine of bureaucratic service to China had resulted in the ascent of the West's most efficient bureaucrats to the top of a service in the climate of which they thrived. The popular, cooperative and well-respected Edwardes, an administrative high-flyer under Aglen, appeared to be just the man to energise this service with youthful leadership and to maintain its confidence in the difficult times which lay ahead, while keeping one eye on the Legation for a lead in China policy. To ensure that he did not develop the highly controversial reputation of his predecessor, Lampson took the sensible precaution of suggesting Edwardes not undertake the guaranty or service of any further domestic loans.[66] The Service thus looked to be in better shape and closer to British interests than it had been in the last years of Aglen's idiosyncratic inspectorate. However, the view which the Nationalists would take of such developments remained to be taken into account.

---

[66]FO 228/3298/200/140 1927: Lampson letter to Wang Chung-hui of 5 March 1927.

# 4
# The Maritime Customs: In Whose Service?

Robert Hart's success in creating a uniquely cosmopolitan and synarchic bureaucracy lay in part in his conception of a fundamental philosophy of service which was simple to use as a basis of discipline. He was also greatly aided by the fact that the romance of the Orient and the prestige of an imperial career served to attract some extremely bright, able and ambitious men. That none of these high-flyers were Chinese was a constant source of concern for Hart: he built the service up that it might train Chinese, by example, to develop the culture and methods of modern bureaucrats, thereby spreading the gospel of altruism, dedication and impartiality throughout the Chinese governmental apparatus. The dream was never achieved in Hart's lifetime, and while Aglen paid lip-service to the idea, he evidently saw close cooperation with Chinese in the Service as a distant goal, to be achieved once the chaos to which he was witness had given way to a more responsible form of government. Chinese employees remained almost exclusively confined to the lowly ranks of the native staff, engaged in the routine assessment and collection of duty rather than administrative office. As a result of institutional inertia and the lack of suitable opportunities for promotion, the Customs elite—the 'Indoor Staff'—was reserved for able European administrators with a facility for cosmopolitan interaction. The standard set for entry into the Indoor Staff was high, the aim being to select gifted generalists whose faculties were adaptable to the rigours of Chinese commercial life. A thorough health examination was also *de rigueur*.

The main node of recruitment for the Indoor Staff was the London office of the Non-Resident Secretary of Customs. It was through this office that Hart, with the aid of Secretary Campbell, had managed to build up the reputation of the Customs in Britain and beyond. Their voluminous correspondence could provide more than enough material for a lengthy study of the early recruits to the Service.[1] Although by the 1920s the importance

---

[1] See *The I.G. in Peking, q.v.*

41

of the London office had been somewhat diminished, and the calls which the Non-Resident Secretary was obliged to make on behalf of his chief had become somewhat fewer, the first judgment on a man's fitness to apply for the Indoor Staff was generally made therein. Aglen sought to maintain the standard of appointees to the Service by individual vetting of applications and the solicitation of a certain type of candidate: "the public school boy of character, who has made good, is the type I want to attract."[2] In August 1921 Guy Acheson, Non-Resident Secretary from 1918 to 1924, introduced an entrance examination for the Indoor Staff, to be sat by "boys who cannot afford Oxford or Cambridge but would otherwise be in the running for scholarships."[3] The bias towards British recruits in the selection process was hardly unintentional. Aglen declared in 1924 that "the Service has always been 50% British and I intend to keep it at that as long as I am here."[4] Only the threat of taxation of the London staff's Chinese earnings moved Aglen even to consider transferring the office to another European or American city, and in any case "as I do not intend merely on account of this Income Tax decision to alter the proportions of representation in the Customs, it will still be necessary for us to have a recruiting centre in London."[5]

Aglen thus chose to recruit to the Service a class of healthy, intelligent and well-mannered youth with great intellectual capabilities, young men who might be considered to have "personality." The effects of that decision might be gauged by a letter from Edwardes to Maze, the Shanghai Commissioner, in 1927, where he notes increasing nationalist demands for the sinification of the Service and states that the overstaffed junior ranks of the Indoor Staff—presumably many of them Aglen's recruitees—should set about making themselves useful to the Service: if they lost their positions as a result of an unforeseen sinification, they could not expect to be pensioned off by the Inspector-General.[6]

This may provide some indication that by the mid-1920s the Service had lost its way. Although Aglen's rhetoric made good use of nautical metaphor, it is arguable that it could do little more than instil a sense of camaraderie as the standing of the foreigner in China swiftly worsened. The original sense of service of empire had vanished, and much of the mystery of the East had instead become a nightmare of corruption and military anarchy. As there no longer existed much of a sense of China, the exhortations of responsibility for the maintenance of China's credit abroad began to ring an

---

[2]*AP*, Inspector-General's Correspondence: letter from Aglen to Acheson of 4 January 1927.
[3]*AP*, Inspector-General's Correspondence Z 309: letter from Acheson to Aglen of 7 January 1921.
[4]*AP*, Inspector-General's Correspondence: letter from Aglen to Bowra of 17 June 1924.
[5]*AP*, Inspector-General's Correspondence: letter from Aglen to Bowra of 27 May 1924.
[6]*MP* Ia/XX, pp. 71-75: letter from Edwardes to Maze of 26 September 1927.

increasingly hollow note. Feuerwerker notes that a concerted attempt by Aglen to increase the level of Chinese literacy within the Service, though apparently satisfactory to its instigator, failed to bring "authentic" Chinese literacy to all but a dedicated few.[7] He further concludes that "by the twentieth century . . . [the Customs] had become a routinized organisation, with little incremental effect on the bulk of the Chinese economy and only a niggardly contribution toward the training of its eventual Chinese successors."[8]

Such a generalised assessment is not entirely accurate, although in keeping with Feuerwerker's contention that the foreign economic presence in China had a similarly negligible positive or negative effect on her vast indigenous economy.[9] Where the Customs Service was significant to China was in its ability to provide a substantial and fairly constant source of revenue, secure enough to entice foreigners to loan money to China on the presumption that future Customs receipts would provide them with a guaranteed return. Thus the fiscal significance of the Customs outweighed any direct contribution it might have made to the Chinese economy.

The Customs Service of the 1920s was not necessarily the prerogative of bright sons of impoverished British upper middle class families: the majority of the commissioners had been recruited in Hart's heyday and retained many of Hart's values. Nevertheless, the youthful direction the Service was taking was clear. Aglen wrote to Bowra in 1924 that he was transferring A.H.F. Edwardes from his personal staff to Canton, "in order that he can have experience at a large port, on promotion as Commissioner."[10] By this time Edwardes was just forty, the youngest commissioner of a major port in the Service. A grandson of the third Baron Kensington, he had been schooled at Haileybury College, and seemed to epitomise the future of the Service he had joined in 1908: young, patrician, popular and very English. In 1925 he was appointed Chief Secretary of Customs, effectively bypassing many of the more qualified commissioners and thereby gaining a reputation as Aglen's hand-picked successor.

Hart was noted for the provisions he made for his extended family in the Service, a nepotistic trait negated, according to Lester Little, by the very high standards Hart set his employees.[11] In 1891 Frederick Maze, his nephew, was appointed as 4th Assistant B in Chefoo, thus joining two of his brothers in the Service. There is no record of the direct effect of Hart's

---

[7] Albert Feuerwerker, *The Foreign Establishment in China in the Early Twentieth Century* (Ann Arbor, Mich.: Center for Chinese Studies, The University of Michigan, 1976), p. 70.
[8] *Ibid.*, p. 72.
[9] *Ibid.*, p. 79.
[10] *AP*, Inspector-General's Correspondence: letter from Aglen to Bowra of 21 August 1924.
[11] Lester K. Little, "Introduction", in *The I.G. in Peking*, vol. I p. 24.

nepotism on the careers of his relations, though it is probably reasonable to assume that young Frederick felt obliged to prove his own worth. Hart's admonition to his nephew, entrusted with opening the new treaty-port at Kongmoon in 1904, was that "your tenure of this responsible appointment will depend upon the manner in which your reponsibilities are discharged."[12]

Responsibility was perhaps the motif of Maze's early career. He appears to have been able and competent in the exercise of his duties, and by 1910 had earned the position of Commissioner in Canton. Although the revolution against the Manchus was born in Hankow, its cradle was Canton, and Maze's despatches to Peking give observant and sympathetic accounts of the epochal movement. It was in Canton that Maze met Sun Yat-sen, and took advantage of his position both as Commissioner of Customs and as an influential member of the foreign community to cultivate the genius of the revolution in that brief moment in which the foreign establishment in China held him in respect. Maze invited Sun to a garden party at the Commissioner's house to introduce him to British Canton, and reported that Sun had stayed for almost two hours.[13] The two men were subsequently to discuss arrangements for the improvement of Canton harbour, an endeavour in which Sun had some interest and Maze some expertise. In addition to its revenue-collecting duties, the Customs Service functioned as a coastguard and harbour-management authority for all of China. Maze's papers show him to be dedicated to schemes of harbour improvement in whichever port he served, and although it is difficult to compare his record in this field with those of other commissioners, his technical capacity and genuine interest in the subject indicate a practical and functional frame of mind not necessarily in keeping with those of the "gifted amateurs" Aglen was recruiting to the Service.

In attempting to strike up a relationship with the revolutionary regime in Canton, Maze was doubtless trying to take an interest in what he considered to be a movement of China's future. It is possible, though not likely, that he foresaw the course of events completely enough to know that the acquaintances he impressed in Canton in 1912 would be the men vying for the balance of power in Nanking in 1928. What is more likely is that Maze was developing concerns for the future of China which clashed with the conventional treaty-port wisdom. Instead of dictating to these people how their country should be run (a premise which was never sanctioned by Hart), he was advising them on the course of material development they had to undertake to render China strong and independent. This is not to mark

---

[12]*MP* Ib/I: instructions from Hart to Maze of 20 February 1904.
[13]*MP* IIa/I: S/O letters 51 and 54 from Maze to Aglen of 12 May and 9 June 1912.

Maze out as a self-conscious paragon of synarchic virtue, but merely a man who had developed a very strong concept of responsible service to an idea of China. The term 'synarchy', and its development in relationship to foreign control of Confucian China, would have been alien to Maze, although he might have appreciated Fairbank's analysis of his uncle's role as a mediator.[14] Maze's efforts in this field were hardly consistent with Aglen's presumptions of superiority.

The tensions which existed between a British servant of the Chinese government and the British mercantile community which he was in theory obliged to protect became ever greater as the central authority which claimed to direct the actions of the Customs Service grew increasingly ghostly. Aglen had taken the lead in deciding the impartial role the Customs was to play in warlord China—yet by claiming to take the Service out of politics he was plunging it into a deeper controversy, that of the nature of constituted authority in China. He could doubtless justify his right to decide the fate of the Service and might even have been inclined to quote from the experience of Hart to support his view. As has been seen above, Aglen's view of the political situation required him to take a strong leadership position, thereby making the Customs as presently constituted indispensable to China.[15] His pronouncements, however, showed that he was intent on making this bureaucratic institution into a self-perpetuating service with an increasingly self-defined and self-referential *raison d'être*.

I have long felt that our continued usefulness, if not safety, as a Service depends on obtaining some administrative share in government finance . . . Such a scheme would have a bonding or unifying effect.

The only thing for me to do is to retire into my shell and sit tight. No money that I control can be got without my signature. The Chinese Government cannot get my signature against my will. The only way in which money could be got would be to relieve me and obtain somebody else's signature and they are not yet prepared to take this step. When they are prepared to do so of course they will do so, and

---

[14]For synarchy, see above, p. 25.

[15]When the Tariff Conference of 1925 proposed the replacement of *likin* by a 5 per cent export tariff, Aglen was delighted: "I can see no other result from what is going on now than an enormously increased prestige and responsibility for the Maritime Customs. There will be tremendous snags, of course, in the South, but some means will have to be found of getting over them." *AP*, Inspector-General's Correspondence: letter from Aglen to Bowra of 28 December 1925.

they will have to take the consequences which would be in many directions very serious.[16]

This was an attitude not unpopular with the British community in China, however much it may have incensed London bankers such as Sir Charles Addis who were trying to negotiate a different financial future for the nation. Aglen's informal role as the "super-minister of finance" demonstrated a degree of control over Chinese affairs which augured well for the protection of British business interests, as a strong Customs establishment could resist all kinds of formal and informal coercion by Chinese administrations of questionable legitimacy. Yet what authority did the Inspector-General hold to determine the legitimacy of Chinese governments, save a well-developed sense of constitutional morality?

Frederick Maze found himself in no position to judge the Chinese revolution by such standards. Before his arrival in Shanghai in 1926 he had, however, served as Commissioner of Customs in Tientsin and Hankow, where he had had opportunities to observe at closer quarters the modern problems of Chinese society. Maze found less use in debating political questions than in improving China's infrastructure and capacity for trade, again demonstrating his technical leanings. After the Tientsin floods of 1916 he worked on the Hai-ho Conservancy Commission, where the Chihli River Commissioner, W.F. Tyler, considered him "a man of exceptional ability— one who was an administrative engineer . . . a man with a broad vision of what there was to do and how to do it."[17] Upon arrival in Shanghai he threw himself into the supervision of the Whangpoo Conservancy Board and the Shanghai Harbour Authority. In August 1928 he addressed Chang Ching-chiang, Chairman of the Shanghai Harbour Board, thus:

. . . the chief need of China at the present time is improved communications . . . The conservation of rivers, etc., serves two purposes. 1st it facilitates navigation, and 2nd, it helps the farmers by preventing floods. Now the farmers, as a class, are the backbone of China, but unless means are provided for them to transport their produce in exchange for other commodities, their usefulness is restricted! . . . It is clear that the mass of the people of China can never be contented or prosperous unless they can trade freely and safely . . . [18]

---

[16]*AP*, Inspector-General's Correspondence: letters from Aglen to Bowra of 5 August 1924 and 7 May 1926.
[17]W.F. Tyler, *Pulling Strings in China* (London: Constable & Co., 1929), pp. 229-230.
[18]*MP* Ia/II, pp. 190-92: letter from Maze to Chang of 7 August 1928.

While one might quarrel with the didacticism of such an approach, it nevertheless articulated an ethic of service to China which differed greatly from that espoused by Aglen. Maze was less concerned than the latter about the national role of an independent Customs service. In this regard he was fond of quoting a memo of Hart's written in 1873:

. . . although the growth of the Customs establishment has been encouraged, yet it has, with foreign intercourse, been to some extent forced upon China: and moreover, its existence implies that Chinese officials cannot do their own work! It should not be forgotten, therefore, that a foreign-controlled Inspectorate may come to an end: it may flourish, do good work, and be appreciated for a time; but the day must come when natural and national forces, silently but constantly in operation, will eject us from so anomalous a position. Meanwhile we are here to act with and assist, and not to ignore or displace Native authority . . . [19]

There is no evidence that Maze publicly articulated such views during his rise to prominence as an increasingly senior member of the Customs Service. Indeed, to invoke "natural and national forces" in 1925 would be to conjure up images of strikes, boycotts and anti-foreign riots. Maze was, however, endeavouring to articulate an independent vision of his role in China and his responsibilities as a Chinese civil servant. That such views achieved broad consonance with the declared tenets of Chinese nationalism was eventually felicitous, although less discerning members of the British community, who depended upon the Customs Service to defend their interests in the informal empire, found it easier to characterise views such as Maze's as panderings, for personal advancement, to a Chinese political fad.

Aglen's dismissal left Maze as the most senior Commissioner in the Customs Service, and certainly the most experienced. His bureaucratic ability was unquestioned and his knack for getting on with the Chinese unparalleled. He was also fifty-seven years of age. It thus became easy to ascribe the failure to promote him above Edwardes to the fact that he was expected to retire at the usual age of sixty, although Aglen was sixty-two at the time of his dismissal and Hart had finally resigned at the age of seventy-two. That Maze had given no indication of his readiness to retire did not overly trouble Aglen or the Peking Legation in their recommendation of Edwardes. Maze had said and done enough in his Customs career to indicate his opposition to the course which Aglen had taken. While such opposition might have been intellectually acceptable, in a situation where vital British interests were at stake it would not do to tempt fate by appointing a man

---

[19]*MP* Ia/III pp. 4-5: excerpted from a press release prepared by Maze of 10 January 1929.

apparently sympathetic to a dangerous nationalist movement. Thus Maze's name only entered the initial succession debates as one to be kept out, or to be prevented from taking advantage of Aglen's dismissal. Any prejudices about Maze's nationalist leanings were not expressed at the time, although they were later amply elaborated.

In the political arena of informal empire, race and nationality were predominant considerations. Maze, however, had a slightly unconventional racial and national background. Born and educated, as Hart had been, in an Ireland united under British rule, this Ulsterman was not necessarily able to find a natural community of interest with the Anglocentrism with which British society in the treaty ports was permeated. Although from Scots Protestant rather than Celtic Catholic stock, and therefore not necessarily drawn to the Irish nationalist cause, Maze's background would, nevertheless, hardly have fitted him to mingle closely with the English majority in social settings such as Holy Trinity Cathedral.

In fact, upon his arrival in Shanghai he became a prominent member of the St. Patrick's Society, serving as president in 1927. The objectives of the Society were stated to be : "1. The relief of Irishmen or their families when indigent or in difficulties. 2. The promotion of goodwill and friendship amongst Irishmen in the Far East."[20] Maze waxed quite lyrical over the influence of the Irish in Chinese affairs in his Presidential Toast at the society's Annual Ball in March 1927. He cited the names of Sir John Jordan, Sir Robert Hart and Sir Robert Bredon as men who had "extensively participated" in the development of Anglo-Chinese relations, discreetly omitting his own familial relationship to the latter two.[21] His invocation of the patron saint of the society indicates the role in which he envisaged himself in China:

> Unlike most of the other Patron Saints, [Saint Patrick] lived and worked in the country of his adoption. He was not an absentee Saint! And when he finally left Ireland, where he displayed patience, wisdom and courage, it was a happier and better land than when he entered it![22]

Statements such as this indicated to Shanghai expatriate society that Maze was more concerned with his effect on China than his effect on the Shanghai scene. In a community in which the nationalist threat had instilled a more acute sense of self-definition, this was not necessarily a politically

---

[20]From the St. Patrick's Society letterhead: *MP* Ia/II, p.280.
[21]Bredon, a previous nominee for the post of Inspector-General, was Hart's nephew and thus Maze's cousin. See below, p. 70, n. 29.
[22]*MP* Ia/II, pp. 34-35.

astute position to take.[23] Yet in his graceful articulation of the distinctly ambivalent position of an Ulsterman whose country was half-released from British rule, Maze was able to demonstrate his aim: not to glorify his surrogate mother-country by what he could achieve in the pursuit of its name and its values, but rather to honour his upbringing, family, training and homeland by giving as much of it as he could in the service of his adoptive home.

---

[23]For the Shanghai response to the nationalist threat, see Nicholas R. Clifford, *Spoilt Children of Empire*.

# 5

# Dual Control

To judge by the nature of their Semi-Official correspondence, the working relationship which Maze and Edwardes struck up was initially a healthy one.[1] Yet deep resentments were soon to emerge as the conflicting opinions of the two men on the direction of the Service were laid bare by the increasing irresistibility of the Nationalist Government. Maze was Edwardes' senior in experience and training, if not status: he might reasonably have expected his opinion to be influential. His position in Shanghai put him in charge of the greatest single source of Customs revenue, while his long service in the South had made him more than usually acquainted with the motivations and arguments behind the Nationalist cause.[2] Edwardes was swiftly to be acquainted with the plans Maze had for a Customs Service in a divided China.

On 25 May 1927 Owen O'Malley, now Counsellor at the British Legation, reported a conversation with Edwardes in which the latter had said he was "fed up with the whole thing." Edwardes had also indicated a belief that Maze and the Hankow Commisioner, Ferguson, were both intriguing to gain the post of Southern Inspector-General.[3] This may have constituted simple paranoia on Edwardes' part: O'Malley stated that Edwardes "is afraid of Maze who has always been regarded as being in the running for the post and is an ambitious and not over scrupulous man."[4]

Edwardes' fears had been crystallised by the formation in Shanghai of a union for Chinese customs employees. On 28th April Maze reported its

---

[1] The Semi-Official correspondence for 1927–28 is found in *MP* vol. IIa.
[2] Conservative estimates put the figure for Customs revenue at Shanghai at forty per cent of the total collectible revenue.
[3] FO 228/3590/5A/3 1927: O'Malley minute of 25 May 1927.
[4] *Ibid.*

objectives to include public agitation for the recovery of Customs autonomy, the increase of the qualification standard for Chinese staff to enable them to take high-ranking posts in the Service, and the reform of the Customs system the better to serve China.[5] Maze blamed this phenomenon on the excess of idle Chinese tidewaiters on the Shanghai staff. The movement was undoubtedly also galvanised by the recent arrival of the Nationalists in Shanghai, although the Kuomintang had recently been purged of its communist elements and the radical element of the General Labour Movement had been crushed. The main drive of this union appeared to be towards the rapid sinification of the Service, a principle which Edwardes recognised as legitimate but unattainable under present conditions:

> Sinification of the Service is bound to come, in fact it is progressing steadily all the time: but attempts by so-called Customs Unions to hasten that process unduly, and to force the hands of the recognised Head of the Service can end only in disaster. Be careful to have nothing to do officially with any such union.[6]

While Edwardes paid lip-service to the ideal of sinification, he had hardly welcomed it with open arms. Such an attitude was consistent with Edwardes' previous communications with Maze on the subject of nationalist stirrings within the Customs. The entry of the Nationalists into Shanghai had been the occasion of a one-day strike, towards which Maze had been indulgent:

> The Nationalist entry into Shanghai is, of course, a political event of the first magnitude, and I find it quite natural that Chinese members of the staff, especially the Cantonese, desired to participate in the celebration of such an important occasion.[7]

Maze had also been of the opinion that it was better for Customs employees to form their own union than to join the General Labour Union, as this made it easier for the foreign staff to exert their influence over it. He concluded his despatch with a statement of policy:

> I ought to try to make it clear that it is quite impossible for us to stop, or even to check, the spirit of nationalism (which fundamentally is justifiable) which now prevails and with which a large section of our Chinese staff is imbued—the most that we can do is to strive to guide it on safe lines as far as we are concerned, and restrict it to safe limitations, and this is the policy which I am following. I request you

[5]*MP* IIa: S/O cable 740: Maze to Edwardes of 28 April 1927.
[6]*Ibid.*: Edwardes to Maze of 11 May 1927.
[7]*MP* IIa: S/O cable 722: Maze to Edwardes of 25 March 1927.

kindly either to confirm this policy, or else to communicate another definite line of action for me to adopt.[8]

Edwardes replied by conceding rather than embracing Maze's point: the Customs should eschew challenges to nationalist sentiment in order to avoid the appearance of "taking sides" with "imperialism." Yet he refused to sanction the cause of nationalism as Maze had: "Individuals in the Service must, of course, be allowed to hold whatever political opinions they please: but they must not allow the expression of, or action on, those opinions to compromise the service, the safety of which lies in steering clear of politics."[9]

Maze did not grant the union official recognition. He did, however, arrange for the Bank of China to deduct one per cent of the pay of each Chinese staff member, the sum to be remitted to the union as dues, as requested by Yü Fei-pang, the Superintendent of Customs at Shanghai.[10] Edwardes was furious at this slight to his authority and judgment. In his view, Maze had thereby given the union recognition, and he said as much in his reply. He nevertheless intended to "defer to [Maze's] judgment." Maze replied in defence of his position, stating that he had no power to override the Superintendent: the new Customs Association was an outgrowth of the nationalist movement and could not be quelled.[11] It was on receipt of this cable that Edwardes told O'Malley of his fears, referring to the Shanghai Commisioner's "open defiance" and what he took to be a threat by Maze that to open the question of recognition might lead the new Nanking government to question Edwardes' credentials as Acting Inspector-General.[12] Whether or not Edwardes thought he was being bullied, he unhappily acquiesced in Maze's opinion, and when O'Malley offered the services of the Legation as a means to exert pressure on Maze, Edwardes waved it away.

It is probable that the establishment of the Nationalist government at Nanking was giving Edwardes cause for concern. Unable to leave Peking to negotiate his position with the South for fear of suffering the same fate as Aglen, he was reduced to applauding the overtures which Maze had been making on the Customs' behalf to Chiang Kai-shek and the Bankers' Association of Shanghai.[13] He had been making strenuous efforts to

---

[8]*Ibid.*

[9]*Ibid.*: Edwardes reply to Maze of 2 April 1927.

[10]*MP* IIa: S/O cable 746: Maze to Edwardes of 16 May 1927.

[11]*MP* IIa: S/O cable 751: Maze to Edwardes of 25 May 1927.

[12]FO 228, *loc. cit.*: Maze, however, had not made the threat at all explicit in his communications.

[13]*MP* IIa: S/O cables 723, 725: Maze to Edwardes of 28 March and 30 March 1927.

influence the "Chinese who count": he was "fortunately . . . on good terms with them all."[14] The chaotic nature of communications with the North in the days before the fall of Shanghai had also led to Maze's functional independence: when Chinese officials of the Customs were unable to contact the Inspectorate-General, they relied on Maze for information and instructions.

The precariousness of this position appeared to prey upon Edwardes. He asked O'Malley whether the Legation would support his claim to his office after the Nationalists reached Peking, "as he thought most likely," and was reassured by an emphatic affirmation. The question of the Customs succession was thus broached to the British diplomatic community. O'Malley had the perspicacity to note that a competing claim from another Briton would create a rather difficult situation, and immediately telegraphed Lampson, who was in Shanghai:

> O.I.G. states very confidentially that both Ferguson and Maze are intriguing to get appointment as I.G. from Southern government and that latter has lately shown himself insubordinate and untrustworthy. He does not wish us to do anything about this. This telegram is only to put you on your guard in conversations with Maze.[15]

One can only hypothesise as to the origin of Edwardes' concerns. Certainly he may have been intimidated by the tone and content of his subordinate's telegrams. His informal correspondence with Luigi de Luca, the head of the Customs' Statistical Department at Shanghai, may also have alerted him to potential problems. De Luca was Edwardes' candidate to replace Maze at Shanghai at such time as the latter should go on leave or retire; he evidently held the trust of Edwardes above Maze's *protegé*, W.R. Myers, and quite blatantly acted as Edwardes' informant in matters regarding the A.I.G's standing in the Shanghai Customs House.[16]

Maze's papers from this period merely show that he was striving to do his job as best he could under trying conditions. The main cause of jealousy, as he depicted it, was the facility with which Maze dealt with

---

[14]Maze's contacts in Shanghai and Nanking politics were based upon his acquaintance with the so-called "Kwangsi clique" of moderates who had been prominent in Cantonese government after the Revolution; for example, Hu Han-min, C.C. Wu and Sun Yat-sen's son Sun Fo. These important connections gave him a potential for developing Chinese contacts that Edwardes could not hope to match from Peking: moreover, Maze's sympathetic attitude towards the nationalist movement undoubtedly carried *cachet*.

[15]FO 228/3590/5A/3 1927: O'Malley telegram to Lampson (Shanghai) of 26 May 1927: copied to F.O.

[16]*MP* Ia/XX: Edwardes letter to Maze of 26 September 1927 regarding the latter's application for leave. Edwardes subsequently showed messages from de Luca to the Legation as apparent proof of Maze's intrigues.

Nationalist politicians and prominent business figures, his self-conscious sympathy for the nationalist movement, and his refusal to coerce or otherwise undercut his immediate superior, the Shanghai Superintendent. Perhaps Edwardes was entitled to exercise caution when he found Maze showing more deference to the position of his Chinese colleague on the spot than he was to that of his British superior in Peking. In alerting the Legation to this situation, however, he had made sure that Maze's subsequent behaviour would receive close attention. Meanwhile he was obliged to deal with further dissension within the Service.

In May 1927 L. A. Lyall left his position as Vice-Chairman of the Maritime Customs Commission for the Compilation of Values to take up an appointment at the International Committee on Opium and Drugs in Geneva. The occasion of his departure provoked him to write a blistering despatch to the Inspectorate roundly condemning its stewardship of foreign and internal loans and accusing it of prejudicing the interests of the Nationalists by funding the Peking government.[17] He advocated a swift abolition of the Custodian Bank Agreement and the return of as much of the Revenue as possible to the direct control of the Superintendents of Customs. Under Aglen's policy of contracting internal loans on the security of the Consolidated Fund, he noted, the Peking Government was able to mortgage that revenue for its own purposes for several years to come, leading to a total debt of 242 million dollars exclusive of interest. Lyall noted that a great deal of the money borrowed had in fact been used by the faction in control of Peking at the time to buy armaments to attack the South: "the guaranteeing of these loans by the Inspector General has naturally earned for the Customs Service the hatred of South China."[18] In his opinion, this gravely affected the day-to-day running of the Service in the South, where close cooperation between Commissioner and Superintendent at a port was vital: it also removed much of the goodwill which had previously existed between the Customs and local Chinese authorities.

To the argument that the Inspector-General's guaranteeing of internal loans improved China's credit, Lyall replied that it merely improved the credit of Peking, whose government had "for a number of years been undeserving of any credit, and [had] used its credit merely to enrich its friends and promote civil war." He countered a parallel argument, that the Customs had gained the support of the Chinese financial community through

---

[17]The text of a copy of the memorandum, with Maze's footnote, is in *MP* Ia/II 46-57.

[18]*Ibid.*, 50. Aglen had given assurances that the loans would not be used for military purposes, and for Lyall to furnish proof to the contrary would evidently label him as either a liar or a dupe. See above, p.29.

its securing of loans, by citing the impotence of that community in the face of Aglen's dismissal. In Lyall's opinion, the safety of the Customs could only be secured if the administration returned to Hartian principles and ceased to be responsible for the handling of revenue. This object could be achieved not by unilateral action of the Inspector-General, but by his accession to a future request from the Nanking Government that it should receive the revenue to be collected in the areas it controlled. If this request could not be satisfied, the only solution to the problem would appear to be to split the Service in two, leaving the Chinese banking community to work out the salvation of the internal loans.[19]

Lyall's threat to the authority of the Inspector-General was stark, his sympathy for the nationalist cause unconcealed. He expected that the Nationalists would either gain control of China in short order or continue to be a party to China's division: in other words, he did not envisage any waning of nationalist sentiment or collapse of the Nationalist armies.[20] His sentiments were echoed by Maze, who had approved the content of the memorandum and added a supportive note.

Edwardes declined to dignify the memorandum with an official rebuttal, but he soundly reproved Lyall for his presumption in expressing such views. If Lyall had objected so strongly to the policy of the Inspectorate-General, he should have resigned in 1921 when it was at its full flood: he was now indulging in disruptive tactics which were endangering the livelihoods of those Customs officers who were not fortunate enough to be leaving the Service. Edwardes had been asked by the British Minister to stay on and keep the Customs united as a going concern: his aim was to accrue enough funds to be able to pension off the foreign staff in the fullness of time.[21]

Edwardes had furnished the Legation with a copy of Lyall's despatch and his reply. Eric Teichman, the Chinese Secretary, minuted that the ground here covered was essentially that of the earlier controversy between Aglen, the Legation and the Foreign Office. He feared that the Foreign Office would take the views of Lyall, "one of the shrewdest and best of the Senior Commisioners of Customs," as proof of its having won the argument. Teichman conceded the principle behind the memorandum, but disputed the speed of its application in practice: he was confident that a more gradual approach by Edwardes would achieve similar results and protect "existing interests."[22] In forwarding the correspondence to the Foreign Office,

---

[19]Edwardes had in fact already relinquished the custodianship of the Consolidated Fund: this was, however, not the issue, as the fund still continued to support past loans to Peking.
[20]Lyall's term for the Nationalists was "the Young China party."
[21]FO 228/3590/5E/1 1927: Edwardes letter to Lyall of 7 June 1927.
[22]FO 228/3590/5F/1 1927: Teichman minute of 10 June 1927.

Lampson was equally defensive. He believed that Chinese clerks entrusted with copying the memorandum might have leaked the proposal to split the Customs to the Nanking Government, which had recently floated the idea in the diplomatic arena.[23]

Edwardes' role as Inspector-General was swiftly finding definition. As an official of the Chinese government who maintained with close links to the Legation and the British commercial community, he saw it as his duty to protect the foreign and domestic interests dependent upon the credit of China, while making some reforms with the aim of straightening out the anomalies which Aglen had bequeathed to the Service. Edwardes' views on the progress of the Northern Expedition are unrecorded, but it is possible that, acting as he was with the encouragement and under the protection of the Legation, he was more inclined to disregard the consequences of reunification under the Nationalists. He was, however, now aware that a substantial and influential section of the Shanghai Customs establishment was, rightly or wrongly, fundamentally opposed to the policy of his Inspectorate. If there remained any doubt in Edwardes' mind as to the ultimate allegiances of Maze and Lyall, the subsequent actions of the Nanking government would serve to clarify his vision.

In early June Sidney Barton, Britain's Consul-General at Shanghai, met with C.T. Wang, a former Minister of Foreign Affairs of the Peking government whose nationalist sympathies had led him to move to Shanghai and establish connections with Nanking.[24] Wang had disturbing news: he told Barton that Nanking was no longer prepared to tolerate the situation of a Customs establishment in Peking and would soon be consulting Edwardes about the appointment of an Inspector-General to administer revenue-collection in the South. Despite Wang's assurances that this move would not interfere with the status of loan repayments secured on the Revenue, Barton fulminated against what he called a "fatal and suicidal . . . foolish and unnecessary" plan.[25] When Lampson arrived in Shanghai five days later he took the trouble to call on C.C. Wu, the Nationalist Minister for Foreign Affairs, to assess the seriousness of the proposal. Wu said that nothing had been definitely decided upon. Lampson was nevertheless suspicious, as he had recently broached the subject with Maze and received "practically the same language" in reply.[26] Although Maze had denied any knowledge of an attempt by the South to split the Customs, Lampson "confess[ed] to being

---

[23] *Ibid.*: Lampson despatch to F.O. of 14 June 1927.

[24] For Wang's career, *BDRC* vol. III pp. 362-64.

[25] FO 228/3590/5E/1 1927: Barton wire to Lampson (in Nanking) of 4 June 1927, recounting conversation of 2 June.

[26] FO 228/3590/5A/4 1927: Lampson telegram to F.O. of 7 June 1927.

doubtful of his sincerity; neither his appearance nor attitude impressed me."[27] The Minister could at least take comfort from the assurances of support for the *status quo* which he had received from Japan. The Japanese Minister, Yoshizawa, had been horrified to hear a rumour that the British Legation was planning to support a bid by Maze for the Southern Inspectorate. Lampson was only too happy to correct the impression.[28]

The matter rested for less than a month: at the end of June Maze reported that C.C. Wu had suggested the shift of the Inspectorate-General to Shanghai or Nanking. Lampson was not averse to the idea, as he had wanted Edwardes to travel south to meet with the Nationalists, but Chang Tso-lin forbade Edwardes to leave Peking. Chang's government had also requested that the Diplomatic Body increase tonnage dues to enable the upkeep of China's foreign missions, while at the same time Nanking was taking steps not only to impose the Washington surtaxes on Shanghai, but also to increase tonnage dues "as part of their unbridled campaign of raising funds for their war chest."[29] Lampson found himself in a dilemma: the Northern request was certainly out of order, but he was wary of using the Diplomatic Body to impose a redistribution of revenue. He held that direct diplomatic reapportionment of revenue was contrary to the spirit of the December Memorandum.

There was no direct official communication between the Nanking Government and the Acting Inspector-General: messages for Edwardes were addressed to Maze in Shanghai and subsequently forwarded. Thus on July 6th C.C. Wu asked Maze to send a telegram to Edwardes requesting him to supply estimates for the amounts of tonnage dues and customs receipts which the Ministry of Foreign Affairs could expect to receive. Edwardes failed to answer, and on 12th June Quo Tai-chi, Vice-Minster of Foreign Affairs, requested him to act before the South made "whatever local arrangements [which would be] necessary" to achieve the desired result.[30] This thinly-veiled threat encouraged Edwardes to take his concerns to the Legation. He planned to temporise, and Lampson promised to see what he could do with his "old personal friend" Wu.[31] However Nanking appeared unimpressed by Edwardes' excuses, for on 25 July Maze communicated a further telegram from Wu which read in part:

---

[27]*Ibid.*
[28]FO 228/3590/5E/2: minute by Lampson of 9 June 1927 on conversation with Yoshizawa of 8 June.
[29]FO 228/3590/5A/6 1927: Lampson despatch to Chamberlain of 13 July 1927.
[30]*MP* Ia/II: 58-59.
[31]FO 228/3590/5C/3 1927: Legation despatch to F.O. of 18 July 1927.

The Nationalist Government is dissatisfied with your attitude because you are not obeying orders as you should do. Your refusal to allocate proportionate share of Tonnage Dues . . . now paid to Peking Wai-chiao Pu and also monthly grant to Yangtse Conservancy Committee are test cases. Intolerable to have Government servant overruling its decisions within its territory. If your attitude is persisted in Nationalist Government may be compelled to establish separate Inspectorate of Customs to administer Customs establishments in Nationalist jurisdiction.[32]

Edwardes was stung into a prompt reply:

Maritime Customs Service is a national asset which is endeavouring in the most difficult conditions to maintain China's financial credit abroad which is vital for future reconstruction. The Service is and must remain an entirely non-party organisation, but the Inspector-General, providing that the Loan Service is not interfered with, is quite willing to supply any information to and correspond with the responsible representative of any party and will give every consideration to any request which he is in a position to fulfil. He can see no reason, however, why such correspondence should be discourteous.[33]

He had nevertheless lost ground. On 29 July he received a despatch form Maze which set out a number of demands arising from the latter's meeting with Ku Ying-fen, the Nanking Minister of Finance. The Nationalist Government did not recognise Edwardes as Inspector-General; it requested a territorially proportionate share of all Customs revenues; if this was not obtained, it would split the Service; it would also refuse to ratify all requests for Service moves not sent via the Shanghai Commissioner. Maze reported the great pressure placed on him to acquiesce in the division of the Customs, but made a point of having defended its integrity "at any rate for the time being." He urged Edwardes not to turn down out of hand the request for proportionate revenues: " . . . in equity such a de facto government has claims which seem as strong as those of the so-called Peking 'Government'." In Maze's opinion the Nationalist Government might be rumoured to be on its last legs, but he believed the "Nationalist Party" would maintain its influence and continue to demand a closer control of the Customs Administration, if only for purposes of "face." Maze declared that he was doing his best to maintain the integrity of the Service and to keep the

---

[32]FO 228/3590/5C/6 1927: included in Legation report to F.O. of 26 July 1927.
[33]MP Ia/II: 92-93: Edwardes telegram to Wu via Maze of 26 July 1927.

Inspectorate informed of developments.[34] He maintained, however, that the protests of the Powers were not highly regarded in Nanking, and thus he should be kept informed of the attitude of the Legations towards the future of the Customs.

In fact Lampson was actively considering whether to "submit to *force majeure*" should the Nationalists seize the Southern revenue. In this he was supported by Chamberlain, who found the demand of the South reasonable and believed that, for the good of the Service, Edwardes should drop whatever personal grievances he was nursing.[35] Edwardes, however, reiterated the position that a split in the Service was in nobody's best interests: if Shanghai had its own Inspector-General and collected its own revenue, then it was likely that Hankow, Yunnan or Szechuan would demand the same privileges.[36] In vain he appealed to Chang Tso-lin to be allowed to go south to "stop the rot." Instead he was obliged to stay in Peking and send firm yet conciliatory telegrams to Nanking via the conduit of Maze.[37] When his attempts to effect staff transfers in the South foundered on continued obduracy, he proceeded to authorise the moves unilaterally. As he told Lampson, he did not believe the Nationalists would dare to make trouble.[38]

---

Far from consolidating the position of the Customs and making the confirmation of his appointment a formality, Edwardes ended his first year of stewardship in a decidedly precarious position. Since February 1927 the political landscape had undergone a fundamental change. The Kuomintang was firmly entrenched in Shanghai and was now claiming, with some measure of authority, to have the right to govern the country. Edwardes could not make his way south to come to any kind of understanding with Nationalist politicians, many of whom preferred to deal directly with Maze. It is difficult to tell whether the *de facto* independence from Peking which Maze thus gained was welcome to him. A charitable assumption would be that he merely made the best of the situation according to his principles. It

[34]FO 228/3590/5A/8 1927: Maze letter to Edwardes of 29 July 1927.

[35]FO 228/3590/5C/6-7 1927: Lampson-Chamberlain exchange of telegrams , 26-29 July 1927

[36]FO 228/3590/5A/8 1927: Edwardes to O'Malley and Lampson of 6 August 1927, enclosing Maze's letter of 29 July.

[37]*e.g. MP* Ia/II: 104-05: Edwardes to Wu via Maze of 5 August 1927, maintaining the non-political nature of the Service yet offering to "carry out the reasonable orders of any Government within the sphere of its control." He also endeavoured to demonstrate that the funding of Peking's legations abroad out of tonnage dues constituted the legitimate maintenance of a national asset: *MP* Ia/II: 130: Edwardes to Wu via Maze of 17 October 1927.

[38]FO 228/3590/5A/10 1927: Lampson minute of conversation with Edwardes, 26 September 1927.

has, however, been demonstrated that these principles differed enough from Edwardes' on vital issues such as the legitimacy of the Nationalist cause and the authority of the Superintendent of Customs to give the Acting Inspector-General considerable cause for concern. Maze was making the most of his autonomy to refashion the Customs in ways he felt necessary. In most areas, however, he acted to prevent conflict with the new regime where none should exist, conceding where he felt it worthwhile and sticking fast where it was absolutely necessary.

While one should not necessarily conclude from this evidence that Maze welcomed the Kuomintang with open arms, it would be reasonable to assume that he appreciated its basic programme and sympathised with many of its aims. Perhaps inevitably, then, Maze became the foreign Customs official whom the Nanking Government found most amenable and understanding. His relationship with the Kwangsi clique stood him in good stead—he was swift to send a telegram to C.C. Wu when he heard that the latter had survived an assassination attempt in Singapore.[39] Whether Maze's subsequent tradings on this basic position of trust constituted intrigue on his own behalf or manœuvrings to mould the Service into the form he envisaged is a judgment which is easier to make with a degree of hindsight.

---

[39]*MP* Ia/XX, pp. 98-100: letter of thanks from Wu to Maze of 15 February 1928 in reply to Maze cable of 8 February.

# 6
# The Question of Character

One might consider the increasing rift between Maze and Edwardes to be little more than an internal matter for the Customs, an institution which had sooner or later to come to terms with the bankruptcy of Peking politics and the inexorable march to victory of the Nationalists. Yet to divorce the Customs issue from its wider context at the beginning of 1928 would be to misunderstand the real interests which committed the Legation to Edwardes' succession. By the end of November 1927 the Foreign Office was already anxious over the question. Reporting a conversation with Aglen in November 1927, Chamberlain told Lampson that, in the former's view, to count on Edwardes' appointment was "a dangerous assumption."[1]

In the winter of 1927 the Legation's main concern was not the fact that Maze might mount a serious challenge to Edwardes' eventual confirmation—rather, it was the possibility that the Nanking government might take Customs matters in the South into its own hands, thus depriving the Legation of any effective control over the administration of the Service in the region where British commercial interests were greatest. Moreover, the Japanese Government continued to press its claims for increased Japanese representation, spurred by an apparently mistaken belief that Lampson had promised his support for a Japanese Inspector-General as a successor to Edwardes.[2]

In August 1927, against sustained protest from the foreign business community in Shanghai, the Nationalists had promulgated an independent import tariff which was due to take effect the following month. Although the

---

[1]FO 228/3590/5A/13 1927: Chamberlain cable to Lampson of 2 November 1927.

[2]FO 228/3740/5A/17 1928: Lampson record of conversation with Yoshizawa of 24 January 1928. Lampson was forced to state the British interest in the Customs in quite frank terms, eventually turning to the fact that the question of a Japanese successor to Edwardes was academic as Edwardes was expected to remain in office for sixteen years or more. A letter to Chamberlain of the same date revealed Lampson's fear that the Japanese were attempting to use their support for Edwardes as a lever to gain further advances in the Customs administration.

unilateral imposition of these new surtaxes was cancelled shortly before they
were due to take effect, the threat had galvanised Shanghai diehards into
characteristic defiance:

> We have said that once as important a group of treaties as those
> regulating the Chinese tariffs and safeguarding the loans secured upon
> them were openly flouted by one conspicuous group of Chinese
> political freebooters, the other treaties might just as well be twisted up
> for use as bottle stoppers, and unless drastic action is taken in this
> case we shall see this statement justified within three months.[3]

The cancellation of the tariff gave the *North-China Herald* cold
comfort, for, as it pointed out, the Nanking government was still collecting
the Washington surtaxes which Britain had unilaterally sanctioned in
January.[4] Maze had refused to sanction a plan mooted by Barton whereby
the surtaxes could be evaded by releasing cargoes without the authority of
the Shanghai Superintendent. As he pointed out in a letter to the chair of the
Shanghai General Chamber of Commerce, he was not in a position to
jeopardize the Customs establishment in South China by actively flouting
orders from the *de facto* government via its Superintendent of Customs.[5]
Nevertheless Maze had used whatever influence he had with Nanking to
have the new tariff cancelled or deferred. In a letter to Cheng T'ien-ku,
Chairman of the Tariff Autonomy Commission, he stated that the proposed
tariff was prohibitively high and would discourage Shanghai trade, while
insufficient notice had been given prior to its imposition. Maze's
constructive criticisms stopped short at entering into the debate over the
government's right to impose the new tariff: "the political aspect of this
question does not come within the Commissioner's province, and he
therefore refrains from . . . commenting upon affairs which do not concern
him."[6]

Maze took the precaution of bypassing the Legation and informing
the Foreign Office directly of his stance on the taxation question. The
economic specialist of the Far Eastern Department, Frank Ashton-Gwatkin,
commented that "this correspondence seems to be a kind of re-insurance on
the part of Mr. Maze. He wants to be certain that he gets a fair hearing

[3]Editorial, "The Arbitrary Tariff", *NCH* (13 August 1927), pp. 270-71: originally published in
*NCDN,* 11 August 1927.
[4]Editorial, "Supertaxes and Surtaxes", *NCH*, (10 September 1927), p. 437: originally
published in *NCDN,* 5 September 1927.
[5]*MP* Ia/II, pp. 108-112: letter from Maze to E.T.Byrne of 25 August 1927.
[6]FO 371/12414/90-91: F7194/3/10: Maze letter to Cheng of 23 July 1927, copied by Maze to
F.O. 28 July.

here."[7] Pratt was confident that the "restraining influence" of Maze would lead to the withdrawal of the taxation proposals, and George Mounsey regarded Maze's arguments as "very sound."[8] The eventual abolition of the tariff thus increased Maze's standing, and Pratt wrote both to congratulate him and to solicit his views on Customs issues.[9]

The Legation was less impressed with Maze's influence and perspicacity. Lampson had earlier been encouraged to consult Maze on the taxation issue, but declined in haughty terms:

> From one or two remarks which I have let fall you will realise that I am not satisfied as to Maze's *bona fides* and think that he may be playing up to the Nationalists in the hope of becoming Inspector-General of Customs for the South. I consider Edwardes' opinion is in any case more valuable and do not therefore propose to pursue your idea of consulting Maze unless you press it.[10]

Pratt did press the point: he had been informed of "nothing more than a vague suspicion" that Maze was involved in intrigue, and considered this to be insufficient justification for a failure to consult him. In fact, he warned, a refusal to draw Maze in might make him hostile to Legation policy. He noted the correctness of Maze's approach to the taxation question and suggested that the Legation might encourage the Shanghai Consul, Barton, to keep in close contact with Maze to relay his views to the Foreign Office.[11] Given the friction which had existed between Barton and Maze since their conflict over the surtax affair, the choice of liaison may not have been a particularly good one.

Maze apparently felt increasingly isolated and misrepresented in Shanghai: on 13 September he wrote to Viscount Gort, who earlier that year had been in Shanghai with the Defence Force, asking him to intercede with "some responsible Foreign Office official who might be interested to learn the delicate position in which I have been placed . . . "[12] Pratt eventually received the letter, and minuted "[Maze] thinks that he has not been fairly judged by Shanghai or his views or reasons for his action properly represented to the Foreign Office." While Pratt again mentioned the rumours

---

[7]FO 371/12414/87: F7194/3/10: Ashton-Gwatkin minute to Maze despatch of 28 July 1927.
[8]FO 371/12414/34-64: F7129/3/10: minutes on Nanking tariff proposals, 27 August 1927.
[9]FO 371/12414/87: F 7194/3/10: Pratt letter to Maze of 12 September 1927.
[10]FO 371/12414/70: F 7151/3/10: confidential letter from Lampson to F.O. of 28 August 1927.
[11]FO 371/12414/77: F 7151/3/10: letter from F.O. to Lampson of 31 August.
[12]*MP* Ia/II pp. 119-20: Maze letter to Viscount Gort of 17 September 1927. Gort's brief stay in Shanghai is chronicled in John Rupert Colville, *Man of Valour: The Life of Field-Marshal The Viscount Gort, VC, GCB, DSO, MVO, MC* (London: Collins, 1977), pp. 60-63.

of Maze's intrigue, he refused to countenance them without further substantiation.[13]

A disturbing disjunction had thus arisen between the views of the Legation and those of the Foreign Office on Customs affairs. Differences of opinion over Customs affairs had existed between the two bodies for some time, as accounts of Aglen's Inspectorate illustrate.[14] However, those differences had stemmed from the lack of a definite or effective British policy to address the nationalist threat and the increasing anarchy in China. As one of the architects of the December Memorandum, Lampson had probably been sympathetic in theory to the eventual need to surrender the administration to Chinese control. However, he was now 'on the spot', faced with a situation in which the Nationalists had effectively divided the country in two and threatened to do the same to the Customs Service. The Legation was practically powerless to prevent such interference, having in principle recognised the justice of the nationalist cause. Thus it could only rely on Edwardes' rhetoric of unity and stability to preserve the administration intact.

Lampson had openly encouraged Edwardes to take the position of Acting Inspector-General in the British interest, and was sustaining Edwardes' resolve through personal friendship.[15] He thus created a bond between the perceived interests of the Legation and the Inspectorate-General to which neither Hart nor Aglen had aspired. From this perspective Maze's independence must have appeared particularly threatening, particularly given the rumours of his character and ambition. For him to mount or to sanction a Nationalist challenge to the integrity of the Customs (actions of which he was believed capable) would inevitably weaken and embarrass the Legation.

Maze himself appears to have been attempting to establish a *modus vivendi* with the Nationalists for the purposes of maintaining the effective functioning of the Customs in the South. This was not an interpretation which the Legation was prepared to place on his actions. His opening of an independent channel of communication with the Foreign Office may have been caused by mistrust of the Peking diplomatic establishment and his unpleasant experiences with Barton. His overtures created a far better impression with the officials of the Far Eastern Department who felt that it was better to manage the Nationalists through a policy of cooperation than

---

[13]FO 371/12415/218: F 8389/3/10: Pratt minute of 2 November 1927 to letter from Maze to Gort, *q. v.*

[14]For example, Eugene Byrne, *The Dismissal of Sir Francis Aglen* (B.A., Modern Languages: University of Westminster, 1993)

[15]The two families frequently dined together, played tennis and went to the races, and Edwardes assumed the role of Father Christmas at the Lampson's children's party in December 1927 (recorded in *KD* f.117r (1927): Saturday December 24th 1927).

through one of conflict. Here policy and diplomacy clearly diverged, for it was apparent that the Legation lacked confidence in this expression of even-handedness. In the intensifying conflict between North and South there existed no universally-recognised neutral ground. Although British policy was predicated on the eventual success of the Nationalists, there was nevertheless a clear difference of opinion between policymakers and diplomats as to how soon their forces would achieve supremacy and form a government which was deserving of official recognition.

Maze's entreaties to the Foreign Office, although favourably received, had raised a degree of suspicion. In October 1927 he wrote that the Nationalists had offered him the position of Southern Inspector-General, which he had refused. Pratt noted the correctness of his attitude, but was also aware of a creeping ambition: " . . . he resents the appointment of Edwardes as Acting Inspector-General over his head and would no doubt seize any chance of becoming Inspector-General in his place." Pratt had taken the precaution of discussing Maze's case with the Customs Non-Resident Secretary, J.W. Stephenson, and was informed that Edwardes was not the only object of Maze's jealousy: when Stephenson had been appointed Chief Secretary at the Inspectorate in 1925 Maze's resentment had been plain, although his attitude to Stephenson had been "strictly correct." Consequently Pratt formed the opinion that " . . . however much [Maze] may wish to be Inspector-General he will never gratify his ambition at the expense of the Service or of the public interest." A survey of Maze's views on Customs issues, including his support of Lyall's memorandum, led Pratt to conclude that "Maze would make a better Inspector-General than Edwardes, who is unfortunately committed to the Aglen policy in these matters."[16]

The new year was ushered in by Lampson's renewed attempt to establish Edwardes as substantive Inspector-General. He reported that the Peking government was prepared to confirm the appointment as soon as Aglen's deferred resignation became effective: however, "well-informed sources" had reported that Maze was definitely involved in intrigue with Nanking.[17] Lampson reiterated Edwardes' suitability for the post and the potential for disloyalty of Maze. He had, however, instructed Barton to "appeal to Maze as a loyal British subject with the welfare of his service at heart."[18] The Foreign Office reaction to this communication was mixed. William Strang believed that "the Peking group seem to have got their knife

---

[16]FO 371/12415/323-24: F 9053/3/10: Pratt minute of 29 November 1927 to Maze letter of 20 October.
[17]Lampson's diary for 3rd January records an interview with Edwardes during which the latter "made no secret of the fact that he regarded Maze—and had long done so—as disloyal both to himself and to the Customs Service." KD f.1v (1928): 3 January 1928.
[18]FO 228/3740/5A/2 1928: Lampson cable to F.O. of 4 January.

into [Maze] . . . in Customs matters, as in other things, Peking and Shanghai do not easily see eye to eye." Ashton-Gwatkin stated that Edwardes' solid service throughout 1927 merited British support, though not at the expense of "civil war" within the Customs. Mounsey found the Maze issue to be "embarrassing," but believed that Barton's appeal to his loyalty would serve as a litmus-test of his intentions.[19] Chamberlain, whose close working relationship with Lampson inclined him to trust the latter's instincts, gave unqualified approval to his attitude despite the misgivings expressed above.[20]

Maze's interview with Barton was revealing, but not in the positive manner Mounsey had expected. The Shanghai consul reported that Maze had turned down the offer of the Southern Inspectorate in July 1927, but that he remained firm in the opinion that a split might be inevitable if the existing administration failed to win the confidence of the South. Most of the dissatisfaction to which he referred concerned Edwardes' refusal to remit a proportion of the Customs revenue to Nanking, but there was also residual discontent with his close connections to Aglen's policies. The only way to maintain Customs integrity was either to deny Edwardes confirmation or to move the Inspectorate to Shanghai. Barton was impressed neither by Maze's message nor by his attitude, and took the latter's references to prominent Nanking figures to indicate that his relationship with the South was closer than was proper.[21]

The Legation continued to take Edwardes' word over that of Maze. Chinese sources were apparently delivering reliable reports of Maze's pandering to the South. Wang Ko-min, a former Minister of Finance at Peking, a former governor of the Bank of China and a man with close ties to both the Peking and the Shanghai banking elites, had intimated to Edwardes that the South would "tacitly acquiesce" in his confirmation by the North if he would come to Shanghai before the end of January.[22] This evidence of Southern receptiveness contrasted sharply with previous impressions, and Edwardes seized his chance. On 27 January the newly-appointed Nationalist Minister of Finance, T.V. Soong, had formally declared tariff autonomy on behalf of the Nanking Government and had asserted the right to control of the Customs revenue proportionate to the sixty-five per cent of territory which the Nationalists claimed to control. Edwardes had planned to depart on 28 January, and in fact was reported as having done so, although on the

[19]FO 371/13194/1-2: F 46/46/10: F.O. minutes to Lampson cable of 4 January, *q.v.*
[20]FO 228/3740/5A/6 1928: Chamberlain cable to Lampson of 4 January 1927.
[21]FO 228/3740/5A/7 1928: Barton wire to Lampson of 6 January 1928.
[22]FO 228/3740/5A/8 1928: A.F. Aveling minutes of meeting with Edwardes, 11 January 1928. For Wang, *BDRC*, vol. III.

31st he was still in Peking, preparing to ignore a governmental order forbidding him to travel.[23]

The invitation to Edwardes, whether formal or informal, had apprently served to discredit Maze's insinuations that the former was not *persona grata* in the South, even though Soong declared that Edwardes was visiting him in a "purely private capacity" and the Deputy Minister of Finance, Quo Tai-chi, stated not only that Edwardes was "self-invited," but that Maze himself was most definitely *persona grata*.[24] Edwardes had stated that he would only seek confirmation if approved in some form by both Northern and Southern governments. His invitation south indicated that there were elements working in his favour. This led to the conclusion that Maze must have been involved in intrigue with other elements of the Nanking Government. Lampson's tone was becoming increasingly stern, as he began to make dark threats about "imposing our will" in Shanghai "should matters come to a head."[25] He also proposed that diplomatic representatives of Britain and Japan formally inform Nanking that Edwardes had their official backing and that "H[is] M[ajesty's] G[overnment] disapproved of attempts being made by the Nanking authorities, who more than ever have no claim to be considered a government, to oust Edwardes in favour of Maze."[26] Lampson was apparently incensed by what he considered Nanking's "absurd" claim of control over sixteen provinces, though he conceded that "it is equally true that Peking do [sic] not control them."[27] The implication was that for the time being the Customs was only safe under impartial control—the best man to exercise such control, of course, being Edwardes.

Barton interviewed Maze again between 12 and 15 February, this time because Edwardes had complained that the native staff in the Customs Union had agitated against him on his trip South. It is probable that Barton's questioning was less than diplomatic, but there exists no record of his attitude in Maze's papers. Maze's answers indicate that Barton had impressed upon him his duty as a servant of the Customs to safeguard Chinese and foreign interests, and his patriotic duty as a Briton not to embarrass His Majesty's Government by obstructing the candidate supported by the Legation and the Foreign Office. The digest of the interview recorded

[23]*NCH*, 28 January 1928, p. 126: *KD* ff. 17v-19r (1928): Monday January 30th–Tuesday January 31st 1928.

[24]*NCH*, 18 February 1928, p. 247: FO 228/3740/5A/25 1928, cutting from *North China Standard*, 31 January 1928.

[25]FO 228/3740/5A/31 1928: Lampson letter to Barton of 1 February 1928, copied to Wellesley (F.O.)

[26]FO 228/3740/5A/37 1928: Lampson (H.M.S. Foxglove) cable to Foreign Office via Peking, 13 February 1928.

[27]FO 228/3740/5A/38 1928: Lampson (H.M.S. Foxglove) cable to Shanghai, 14 February 1928, repeated to Peking.

Maze as saying that the South was justified in treating the appointment of an Inspector-General as a domestic issue in which it should have the proportionately greater say; that a Maze inspectorate would not affect foreign loan interests; that the question of patriotism was therefore not involved; and that he had a superior claim to the post which he would not abandon "for nothing." He furthermore offered to retire after his leave if the North would give him an "adequate" pension and the British Government an "adequate" decoration.[28]

There are three interpretations to be placed upon this report. Maze may have been speaking honestly while Barton recorded the conversation accurately. Maze may have presented a case which Barton distorted intentionally or unintentionally. Maze may even have been provoked to exaggeration, exasperation or ridicule of the British pressure upon him. Hindsight would suggest the first of these explanations, for even after the content of Maze's demands became known in Shanghai society the pugnacious Commissioner uttered not one word in rebuttal, although he generally raged against press criticism of his role and character. Whichever interpretation is correct, one imagines Barton almost gleefully recording what can only be described as a huge indiscretion. "Knowing Maze, I am sure that he is incapable of appreciating that view of his action which would describe the latter as sordid or of withdrawing from it. He is in fact following the precedent set up by his uncle Robert Bredon in somewhat similar circumstances."[29]

Shorn of its pejorative flavour and allowing for a fair degree of extraneous misrepresentation, Barton's account probably captures Maze's character and attitude with a reasonable degree of accuracy. The opinion of Stephenson on Maze's ambition has already been noted,[30] and that view had recently been corroborated by L. A. Lyall.[31] Maze's support for the

[28]FO 228/3740/5A/40 1928: Barton letter to Lampson (on tour) of 15 February 1928, repeated to Peking and the F.O.

[29]Ibid. Bredon was the nephew of Sir Robert Hart, his eventual deputy, and the man he initially chose as his successor. The Foreign Office promised Bredon the position of I.G. while negotiations to secure a British succession were being concluded with the Tsungli Yamen in 1898, but by 1904 Bredon's apparent unpopularity in the British community (largely due to his popularity with the Chinese) led the Foreign Office to veto his appointment. The parallels are not at all as extensive as Barton implies, but the implication was enough to have Lampson commission a memorandum on the Bredon case with which to attack Maze (FO 228/3741/5A/78 1928). The case is dealt with tangentially in The I.G. in Peking, especially letters 1285 and 1431. W.F. Tyler suggests that Bredon lacked the altruism and reserve which the position required (Pulling Strings in China, p. 140).

[30]See above, p. 67.

[31]Pratt approached Lyall in early February 1928 to ask him his opinion of both Edwardes and Maze. Edwardes, though fairer than Aglen to the Outdoor Staff, was "extremely obstinate, had poor judgment, and had probably adopted his present policy out of a sense of loyalty to Aglen."

territorial claims of the Nationalists was, however, ideological rather than pragmatic, and was deeply rooted in his conception of the role of the Customs Service. As a man in his thirty-sixth year in China, he was not necessarily likely to feel the full force of a rallying-cry to King and Country, particularly when asked to abdicate his claim to a position of authority to a "fellow Briton" fourteen years younger and with an approach to the Service which Maze considered to be contrary to China's interests. Whether his request for a pension and a decoration was made in all seriousness it was difficult to say, but the receipt of "something more than a C.M.G." would undoubtedly elevate him in Shanghai society and add a certain lustre to his retirement.[32]

Such apparent venality, even if expressed in jest, was sufficient to send shock-waves through the Legation and the Foreign Office. If Maze were paid off, the scandal would destroy British prestige. If he remained as a subordinate to Edwardes, the latter would never be safe, and if he were eventually appointed, he could command no respect whatsoever. Maze had thrown away the considerable amount of sympathy and respect which he had gained in Whitehall over the previous six months. Chamberlain noted that "Mr. Maze has forfeited all claim to respect and should never be allowed to receive any favour at the hand of the King or any respect from us." Mounsey noted a further problem: if Edwardes should decide to withdraw under Nationalist pressure, a third candidate for the Inspector-Generalship would be required. Stephenson was discreetly asked to draw up a short-list for Foreign Office consideration, but none of the British candidates he suggested were as promising in character, age or health as Edwardes. The spectre of a Chinese Inspector-General materialised, accompanied by the sobering possibility of the Japanese Legation attempting to trade on its earlier support for Edwardes to secure the post for its nominee. The only

---

Maze was "a very able man, and with far sounder judgment than Edwardes, but would certainly play for his own hand." Lyall thought that the chances of Maze splitting the Customs were fairly high. FO 371/13194/42-3: F 682/46/10: Pratt minute of conversation with Lyall, 6 February 1928.

[32]The request for "something more than a C.M.G." appeared in Barton's letter to Lampson of February 15 which elaborated on the interview: FO 228/3740/5A/52 1928. The Order of Saint Michael and Saint George is the decoration usually awarded to Britons who distinguish themselves in foreign service, and comes in three gradations: Commander (C.M.G.), Knight (K.C.M.G), and Knight Grand Cross (G.C.M.G.). The fact that Aglen received the G.C.M.G. on his dismissal, outranking the knighthood of the Order of the British Empire (K.B.E.) which he already held, would perhaps account for Maze's stipulation. The *North-China Herald* had noted that Aglen's award was only fitting, given his unstinting service to China and the Chinese ingratitude exemplified his dismissal by Peking. *NCH* (26 February 1927), p. 316.

hope of retaining a British I.-G. now appeared to lie in backing Edwardes to the hilt and cajoling the South into confirming his appointment.[33]

Edwardes was well aware of Maze's attitude, since the latter had made it plain to him on his arrival in Shanghai that there was a "price at which he would be willing to make way."[34] Although Maze had also been at pains to state that nothing personal was involved in his actions, Edwardes drafted a letter of resignation while still in the South. He cited Maze's undermining of the Inspectorate-General in matters not only of Customs policy but of staff relations, and implicitly accused Maze of having turned the majority of the Nanking government against him. Furthermore, he would not be a party to any scheme which involved buying Maze off in such an ignoble fashion.[35]

Edwardes was dissuaded from this course of action only after Legation officials showed him the recent correspondence with the Foreign Office. This served to convince him that he had the effective support of Whitehall and the Legation in his struggle.[36] Nevertheless, his threat had made a considerable contribution to the tension of the situation. In addition to persuading the South of Edwardes' fitness and *bona fides*, British officials now had to nurse the latter's resolve, for the political and diplomatic damage of a resignation on such terms would be catastrophic. Maze had managed to ridicule most accepted notions of a Briton's duty to the maintenance of informal empire, and in doing so had forced Britain into a position of direct challenge to the authority of the Nationalist government.

---

[33]FO 371/13194/47-50: F 819/46/10: minutes to Barton telegram of 16 February 1928.

[34]FO 228/3740/5A/52 1928: Barton letter to Lampson of 15th February 1928 recording conversation with Edwardes.

[35]*Ibid.*: Edwardes letter to Lampson of 15th February 1928, enclosed in Barton letter to Lampson of same date. A rather exasperated Lampson noted privately: "Edwardes . . . seems to be rather playing the goat by rushing in with a premature declaration that he will throw in his hand and resign." *KD*, f. 33r (1928): 15 February 1928.

[36]FO 228/3740/5A/53 1928: B.C. Newton (Peking) cable to Lampson (Canton) of 1 March 1928.

# 7

# Nationalist Politics and the Customs Crisis

Thus far little mention has been made of the role of the Nationalist government in the fight for control of the Customs Service. British views of the fitness to rule of the Nanking regime were jaundiced by reports of continual factional struggles and the failure to achieve a satisfactory settlement of the Nanking Incident. Although there were heartening indications that the wave of anti-British protest had effectively been quelled with the purging of the Communist wing of the Kuomintang and the expulsion of its Russian advisors, the eventual attitude of the Nationalist government towards British overtures for treaty revision had not yet become clear. Moreover, it was suspected in some quarters that below the façade of constitutionality, moderation and reasonable conciliation which Nanking increasingly presented to the Diplomatic Body there churned a seething maelstrom of 'extremism' which would seize on any opportunity to renew the attacks on the position of the foreigner in China.[1]

Despite its continuing mistrust of the nature of the Nationalist regime, the Legation found some reasonable and businesslike figures whom it attempted to cultivate and bolster. Foremost among these was T.V. Soong, whose Methodist faith and Harvard education lent him an air which Westerners could recognise as one of decency. Meyrick Hewlett, who as Consul-General attached to Nanking was the British official in closest touch with Nationalist affairs, described Soong as "perhaps the most outstanding figure in the National Government at that time."

T.V., as he was known to all his friends, was an interesting character. He always struck me as fearlessly straight, and unwilling to let himself be used as a mere money-collecting machine for those in

---

[1]Enumerating to Chamberlain the reasons why Maze's appointment as Inspector-General could not be countenanced, Lampson concluded that "Maze's substitution for Edwardes would be regarded by the extremists of all parties as a victory against foreign influence in the Customs and would thus militate against the future foreign interest in the Service." FO 228/3740/5A/48 1928: Lampson (Hong Kong) despatch to Chamberlain of 22 February 1928.

power. He had the best interests of China keenly at heart, and never favoured wild expenditure on military ventures.[2]

Lampson remarked in his diary that he "found Soong an extremely attractive person . . . unless he is a born actor he is certainly sincere. He struck me as extremely clever and with considerable breadth of outlook."[3] A.D. Galloway, Swire's man in Hankow in 1927, reported that Soong was "very able" and "pro-British," a "well-educated progressive" with an "interesting personality" who "speaks our language faultlessly." In the course of negotiations for a loan from foreign banking interests, Soong had persuaded Galloway that Britain was the nation the Nationalists found best for business, and that British firms should respond swiftly to such overtures lest they be overtaken by the United States or Japan.[4]

The lack of an adequate biography of the brother-in-law of Sun Yat-sen and Chiang Kai-shek naturally hampers attempts to come to terms with his role over the period of the Customs succession crisis. Nevertheless the small amount which can be gleaned from assessments of the first years of the Nationalist era indicates that Soong maintained his outward reputation for plain dealing in the face of immense financial and political pressures. He avoided irrevocable alignment with either wing of the Kuomintang for as long as he could, and as a result earned the suspicion of both the Hankow and the Nanking regimes.[5] Having spent most of 1927 in Japan, he returned to government office in January 1928 with a clear mandate to raise funds for Chiang's revival of the Northern Expedition.[6] During the five-month push on Peking, Soong extracted as much as he legitimately could, while Chiang's extra-governmental associates made up the shortfall in military funding

---

[2]Hewlett, *Forty Years in China*, p. 201. Hewlett did not formally take up residence in Nanking until a satisfactory settlement of the Incident was reached in August 1928.

[3]*KD*, f. 133r (1928): 20 July 1928, after Soong's first visit to Peking.

[4]*JSSP* II 2/6 (box 42) 45(d): letter from B[utterfield] & S[wire] (T.H.R.S[haw], Shanghai) to J[ohn] S[wire] & S[ons] (London) of 8 April 1927, enclosing Galloway telegrams from Hankow of 29 and 30 March.

[5]Parks M. Coble Jr., *The Shanghai Capitalists and the Nationalist Government, 1927–1937*, 2nd. ed.(Cambridge, Mass.: Council on East Asian Studies, Harvard University; Harvard University Press, 1986), p. 31. Soong had the peculiar fortune to be in Shanghai on a reconciliation mission from Hankow at the time of Chiang's April purge of Communist elements, and subsequently had his financial operations in Shanghai severely curtailed. Sterling Seagrave, *The Soong Dynasty* (New York: Harper and Row, 1985) gives a less sober account of Soong's dilemmas (pp. 234-46).

[6]Chiang had withdrawn from government in August 1927 as the Northern Expedition faltered, but was invited to return when it became clear that the succeeding coalition government lacked Chiang's flair for leadership and extortion. Coble, *op. cit.*, pp. 41-44.

through a shameless renewal of the successful extortion campaign of the summer of 1927.[7]

Soong's interest in the development of a stable market economy driven by budgetary responsibility led him to a policy of conciliation with the bruised Shanghai capitalists after the fall of Peking temporarily slaked the Kuomintang's thirst for arms. In his pursuit of Western methods of economic reconstruction Soong appeared all but isolated in a government increasingly riven by factional jealousies and blighted by the priority of immense military expenditures. Coble concludes that Soong courted the capitalists in an attempt to carve out a recognisable political constituency for himself, as well as administering succour to a fiscal golden goose which had been throttled to within an inch of its life.[8] In his pursuit of closer cooperation with business, Soong convened the National Economic Conference in June 1928, thereby creating a prominent public forum in which he could propound his plans for economic reconstruction while also enabling financiers and industrialists to criticise the military establishment. Despite the Conference's threat to withhold loans from the Government unless large-scale disarmament was initiated by the end of July, Soong found the task of initiating capitalist reconstruction increasingly difficult, for Chiang's apparatus of coercion was effectively able to undercut any such ultimatums.[9]

Soong was necessary to the Nanking government, but not indispensable. He had refrained from expressing strong ideological viewpoints which might prove a liability in the highly-charged factional environment of internal Kuomintang politics, though Hewlett remarked that he had a certain intellectual sympathy for the Soviet cause.[10] As Bergère notes, his principal value to the Nationalists lay not in ideological vision or inspirational leadership, but in the creation of the myth of a vibrant and dynamic Chinese political economy:

> Behind the myth created by T.V. Soong for the benefit of his foreign interlocutors, it is today possible to make out a quite different reality—a bourgeoisie subordinated to, and integrated into, the State apparatus, a bureaucracy in a state of flux, uncertain of both its aims and its methods, and a modern economic sector still dominated by the hazards of international circumstances.[11]

---

[7]*Ibid.*, p. 45.
[8]*Ibid.*, pp. 47-49.
[9]*Ibid.*, p. 52.
[10]Hewlett, *op. cit.*, p. 206.
[11]Marie-Claire Bergère, *The Golden Age of the Chinese Bourgeoisie 1911–1937*, tr. Janet Lloyd (Cambridge: Cambridge University Press, 1989), p. 274.

Whether Bergère's interpretation of the reality of the Chinese political economy is accurate, Soong's communication skills were undoubted. As the principal intermediary for foreigners attempting to make sense of the new China, his education, open demeanour and urbanity in dealing with the representatives of the West was invaluable in bringing them into his confidence. For Arthur Young, one of the chief Western economic advisors in the era of Chinese reconstruction, the "ability and resourcefulness" of the main governmental contact of the Kemmerer Commission was impressive.[12] The French statesman Jean Monnet said that "his culture was European."[13] To the British Legation he appeared remarkably free of those supposed proclivities for treachery, intrigue, dishonour, venality and ingratitude with which, in the wearied view of the majority of Britons, Chinese public servants were hopelessly imbued. During the protracted and exasperating negotiations which surrounded Edwardes' attempt to gain the confirmation of the Nationalist government, Soong was never personally criticised by the Legation, and was certainly not subjected to any such slights behind his back. On the contrary, he appeared as a thoroughly decent fellow surrounded by unprincipled rogues, and the longer he survived in what appeared to be a lion's den the greater the Legation's admiration for him grew.

It was Soong who had first invited Edwardes south, creating a personal rapport which subsequent events strained but never severed.[14] His overture to Peking's nominee was unconventional and drew some criticism. Chang Fu-yun, a Harvard classmate of Soong's whom the latter had appointed to the Director-Generalship of the Nanking Kuan-wu Shu, or Office of Customs Administration, stated in his *Memoir* that Edwardes had engineered the visit by approaching Soong with proposals for a joint Tariff Conference involving Nanking and Peking.[15] The prospect of arranging a partition of Customs revenue with the North, which Edwardes appeared to be offering, was appealing to Soong, though Chang indicates that he had an

---

[12]Arthur N. Young, *China's Nation-Building Effort, 1927–1937: The Financial and Economic Record* (Stanford, Calif.: Hoover Institution Press, Stanford University, 1971), p. 338.

[13]For Monnet, Bergère, *loc.cit.*: the reference is from his *Mémoires* (Paris: Fayard, 1976), p. 134.

[14]See above, p. 68.

[15]That Edwardes was initiating overtures towards tariff reform proposals is indicated by a letter he wrote to Maze in December 1927, shortly after the ousting of the Kwangsi clique by the return of Chiang Kai-shek. Although unsure about the composition of the new regime, Edwardes asked Maze "diplomatically" to impress upon the new Minister for Foreign Affairs, C.T. Wang, the necessity of being prepared to negotiate on tariff autonomy: Wang had apparently been magnificently obstructive at the Peking Tariff Conference in 1925–26. *MP* Ia/XX, pp. 90-92: letter from Edwardes to Maze of 13 December 1927.

imperfect grasp of the political and ideological strictures upon him. Soong acted "impulsively and without consulting anyone" in dealing with an official whose authority Nanking did not recognise, appointed by a government with which Nanking was at war, and palpably acting beyond his authority with the evident purpose of maintaining the supra-governmental status engineered by his predecessor.[16] Nevertheless Soong's capitalist backers, for example the Chinese Chamber of Commerce and the Shanghai Bankers Association, were heartily impressed with Edwardes' tariff proposals and encouraged him to push them through.[17]

Soong's readiness to break the Tariff Conference deadlock displayed a bipartisan pragmatism which appeared as characteristic of him as it seemed unusual in an official of the Nationalist government. According to Chang, Soong also opposed a split in the Customs administration, citing reasons (the maintenance of Chinese credit, a bad precedent, a small *pro rata* yield of revenue) broadly consonant with views expressed by the Legation.[18] Yet while Chang grudgingly appreciated this attitude, his account of the resolution of the Customs issue highlights the difference between his principled commitment to Service reform and Soong's opportunism. Even taking into account the many opportunities for rationalisation afforded in writing a memoir from the winning side, it is difficult to mistake Chang's message, loaded as it was with the pieties of nationalist sentiment. Apparently guided by the letter and the spirit of Sun Yat-sen's will, Chang says that he had developed a coherent and radical philosophy of Customs reform based upon the twin objectives of tariff autonomy and native control.[19] While he and Soong agreed that no substantial moves to reform the Customs could be undertaken until Peking fell and the whole Service fell under Nationalist control, he nevertheless appears to have spent the interim in deep consideration of the strategy to be adopted once that moment arrived.

Chang was extremely sensitive to the authority his position conferred. Unlike the Peking Shui-wu Ch'u, which was an independent agency in all respects, the Kuan-wu Shu exercised independent authority only over Customs administration. All matters pertaining to revenue came within the

---

[16]*The Reformation of the Chinese Customs: A Memoir*, in Chang Fu-yun, *Reformer of the Chinese Maritime Customs,* an oral history conducted 1976, 1979 and 1983 by Blaine C. Gaustad and Rhoda Chang (Berkeley, Calif.: Regional Oral History Office, The Bancroft Library, University of California, Berkeley, 1987), pp. 119-20. Courtesy of The Bancroft Library.

[17]FO 228/3740/5A/49 1928: Barton letter to Lampson of 24 February 1928. Edwardes was entertained by the Chamber of Commerce and Bankers Association on 21 February.

[18]Chang, *op. cit.*, p. 116.

[19]*Ibid.*, p. 114.

purview of the Minister of Finance. Such authority which Chang possessed, however, he was determined to assert in the best interests of the Service. He deliberately shunned all formal contact with Edwardes, and was exasperated at Soong's casual dealings with the latter. It was, he said, only good fortune which prevented Soong from inadvertently dealing with Edwardes in an official capacity and thereby recognising his claim to the office of Inspector-General.[20]

Neither Edwardes nor the Legation appeared to be aware of the importance of Chang's position in Nationalist Customs affairs, *soi-disant* though it may have been. He was variously treated and referred to as a subordinate of Soong, "Maze's nominee in the National Revenue Council," and an intriguer who was said to have secured from Maze the promise that he would be Co-Inspector-General in a future Customs administration.[21] Taking into account the possibility that Chang's account may include elements of wishful thinking, or that he may have sought to value his role more highly than Soong did, it is nevertheless clear from reports to the Legation that Chang had, by December 1928, developed a degree of power and influence in his office sufficient for Soong to regard him as a threat and cite his opposition to Edwardes as a hindrance to the latter's confirmation.[22] Chang's role was also obscured by his self-imposed inability to address Edwardes directly: he was reduced to writing drafts of correspondence to be transmitted through Soong.[23] Either Edwardes failed to understand, or Soong failed to make it clear to him, that the Kuan-wu Shu could not ratify Customs appointments submitted by the former. Edwardes was asked to submit lists of Service changes *via* Maze in Shanghai, a formula about which he bitterly complained, declaring that it was tantamount to giving Maze control of the Customs in the South.[24] Chang, however, remained resolute in his refusal to countenance Edwardes' authority as the nominee of the North, and cited the latter's refusal to recognise his authority in this matter as one of the reasons that his confirmation would not be approved.[25]

---

[20]*Ibid.*, p. 124.

[21]*Ibid.*, p. 134: FO 228/3741/5A/135 1928, minute by Aveling of 3 November 1928: FO 228/3741/5A/156 1928, letter from Edwardes to Lampson of 5 December 1928.

[22]FO 228/3741/5A/148 1928: Edwardes letter to Lampson of 25 November 1928, reporting *inter alia* that the Chinese Bankers Association had told him that Soong wished to dispose of Chang but was not powerful enough to do so.

[23]For example, the text of a letter to Edwardes which Chang declares to have been drafted "in my own handwriting" appears in FO 228/3740/5A/73 1928 over Soong's signature. Chang, *op. cit.*, pp. 121-22; letter of 11 April 1928.

[24]FO 228/3740/5A/63 1928: Edwardes letter to Lampson of 29 March 1928. On this occasion Edwardes decided to call the South's bluff and force the appointments through.

[25]Chang, *op. cit.*, pp. 117, 124.

It was a fundamental tenet of Chang's programme as Director-General of Customs that effective reform could only be carried out if the "right man" were appointed Inspector-General. Such a man should be:

> . . . an experienced customs official who had sympathy with the aspirations of the Chinese people for regaining control of the customs and for its reform, who would not be subject to foreign influence, who would cooperate with the Kwan Wu Shu [sic] in carrying out the measures for the reform of the customs service and would unquestioningly carry out the orders of the government.[26]

This description is remarkably coincident with Maze's expressed views on the Customs Service. Chang reinforces this view by noting that he was "in a good position to acquaint [him]self with the past record and attitude towards the Customs" of Maze: he found him "sympathetic" to the aforementioned aspirations, free of inclinations towards foreign influence, cooperative in "handling the delicate situation of a divided customs service" and "rather unique in having received the approbation of the Chinese business community." Such a felicitous meeting of two similar minds was probably too good to be true, and Chang's account may be doubted in the detail. Yet it is important to note that Maze's sympathy towards Chinese aspirations did not spring from nowhere: his battles with Edwardes throughout 1927 had demonstrated his convictions in this regard, while his quasi-independent position was enabling him to direct the Customs as he thought best for China.

Whether Maze had developed his views through genuine conviction, or whether he was opportunistically jumping on the Nationalist bandwagon to gratify his ambition, is one of the central questions which this work attempts to answer. The Legation naturally found it impossible to believe that Maze could entertain such sympathies for the Southern cause without having been promised some reward—hence the accusations of intrigue. As the dispute over the succession dragged on, Maze's perceived function changed. He increasingly came to be seen as a tool and a dupe of the South, liable to be dropped as swiftly as he had been taken up if his requirements became inconvenient. Lampson wondered "whether . . . the South are not deliberately using Maze just as it suits their purpose: I cannot believe that they do not see through him just as much as the rest of us do."[27] His close collusion with the Nationalists was indicative of a lack of moral fibre, while his pandering to a political faction treatened to drag the Service into politics. He was, moreover, held not to be responsive to social conventions or

---

[26]*Ibid.*, p. 117.
[27]*KD*, f. 77r (1928): 23 April 1928.

appeals to honour. Any report in the Press, particularly the Chinese press, favourable to Maze or inimical to Edwardes was immediately attributed to Maze or his "Chinese friends" and his "efficient" handling of propaganda.[28] The campaign of calumny against Maze appeared to continue without any self-consciousness. Maze's renegade status had sanctioned all manner of unpleasantness.[29] One is reminded of the remarks of Edwin Denby, United States Minister to China in the 1890's:

> [The minister to China] is bound to assume that in all cases his countrymen are in the right and the Chinese are in the wrong. It is considered a very strong proof of mental weakness, or moral obliquity, if the minister dares to look into the right or wrong of any question which is alleged to involve the substantial rights of his countrymen.[30]

The ease with which questions involving Chinese politics and society became questions of morality was shown by T.V. Soong's rebuke to Edwardes, who had complained that unsavoury governmental factionalism was preventing his confirmation:

> I have not hesitated to tell you frankly that not every member of the government is in agreement with my conclusion [to confirm Edwardes as Inspector-General], but I cannot emphasize too strongly that it would be unfair to conclude that because those persons for reasons good, bad or indifferent, believe in a different choice, they are

---

[28]*e.g.* FO 228/3741/5A/99 1928: Aveling file-note to Chinese press report of Chamber of Commerce support for Maze over Edwardes, 8 August 1928; FO 228/3740/5A/51 1928, Barton cable to Lampson of 24 February 1928 regarding Chinese press "propaganda" against Edwardes.

[29]Frank Toller of the Far Eastern Department minuted on 31 December 1928: "[This correspondence] seem[s] to indicate that personal feeling is to some extent at the bottom of the Edwardes-Maze trouble. That Maze has acted in a disloyal and dishonest manner is fully established: at the same time Mr. Edwardes' position is not made to look any better when one finds him & the Statistical Secretary [Luigi de Luca, *q.v.*, p.54] discussing how to 'smash Maze' who, after all, is the Statistical Secretary's superior officer." FO 371/13195/344: F 7109/46/10: minutes to Lampson despatch received 29 December 1928.

[30]Charles Denby, *China and her People*, 2 vols. (Boston: L.C.Page, 1906), vol. I p. 91: cited in Albert Feuerwerker, *The Foreign Establishment in China in the Early Twentieth Century* (Ann Arbor, Mich: Center for Chinese Studies, The University of Michigan, 1976) p. 34. Maze was an acquaintance of Denby's son Edwin who was briefly in the Customs Service in the 1890's and later became U.S.Secretary of the Navy: he wrote to Maze to congratulate him on his eventual appointment as Inspector-General. *MP* Ia/II, p. 276, letter of 21 January 1929.

therefore playing politics or dragging a "service" question into politics.[31]

It is necessary, therefore, to remove the prejudiced assumption that because Maze appeared to be in collusion with Chinese interests, his morals were therefore corrupt. Maze challenged one of the prevalent tenets of the psychology of informal empire in China: that Western logic and morality could alone decide the right course for China to take.

Nevertheless, it should not be implied that Maze's actions were inordinately altruistic. Where he saw an opportunity for leverage to achieve his objectives he was not afraid to take advantage of it, and he may have had to abandon some of his scruples to achieve an end which he saw as worthwhile in itself. Thus it is not inconceivable that Maze ingratiated himself with Chang in order to present his proposals for Customs reform, and no less probable that he presented himself as the means whereby such a goal might be achieved. As Chang admits in his *Memoir,* he had no affiliations with the Kuomintang until he was invited to head the Kuan-wu Shu in 1927, and indeed never joined the party. He nevertheless accepted the position of Director-General, but found himself with little to do as the Customs was still in the hands of the Peking Government. It is possible that Chang spent this fallow time in conceiving his grand scheme for Customs reform, but it is tempting to believe that he had a little unacknowledged help from outside quarters. It would be embarrassing for the self-styled "Reformer of the Chinese Maritime Customs" to have to state that his work in restoring the Service to Chinese control was in fact inspired by a foreigner.

When T.V. Soong left the government in 1927 his *protegé* Chang had left with him, to return to the position in January 1928. In the interim the government was staffed mainly by Cantonese moderates of the Kwangsi clique. One of these, Fu Ping-chang, was appointed Director-General of the Shu, and there is evidence that Maze had also made approaches to him. Pratt records a conversation with Fu on the occasion of the visit of Fu, Sun Fo and Hu Han-min to Britain in the summer of 1928. Fu criticised Edwardes' position on the tariff, declared himself dissatisfied with the treatment of Customs native staff, denounced the Aglen policy of revenue control, demanded a return to Hartian principles of Chinese control and made a plea for tariff autonomy. Pratt was astute enough to note that

---

[31]FO 228/3741/5A/110: Soong letter to Edwardes (Shanghai) of 18 September 1928. This icy letter is, however, so much in contrast with Soong's earlier communications with Edwardes that one is tempted to suspect that it was written publicly to establish Soong's credentials as a responsible nationalist. See below, p. 89.

these suggestions tally so closely with suggestions that have been made by the department that I think it advisable to say that they were made entirely spontaneously by Mr. Fu without any leading from me whatsoever. I am inclined to think that Mr. Fu must have got some of these ideas from Mr. Maze, with whom he has frequently discussed these problems.[32]

In case this implicit endorsement was not enough, Fu went as far as he could towards making it explicit: Maze "understood and sympathised with the Nationalist movement" while Edwardes did not.

The nationalist movement had thrived on symbolic incidents such as the May Fourth uprising and the May Thirtieth and Shameen shootings. It was not for nothing that the Kuomintang published an official list of "Days of National Humiliation" to encourage public observance and demonstration. Thus the fact that Edwardes had closed the Canton Customs House for one day as a precaution against the Shameen protests became the symbolic rock upon which his campaign to secure full confirmation was to founder. Edwardes, it was revealed, had acted in direct contravention of the orders of his Superintendent, none other than Fu Ping-chang, and the Canton Minister of Foreign Affairs, C.C. Wu. Edwardes issued a strong refutation of some of the wilder rumours which sprung up around the core of the scandal, and implicitly blamed Maze for spreading disinformation about his actions.[33] This had little effect. Wu was sufficiently influential within the Nanking establishment to be able to turn the incident into another *cause célèbre*, while Fu, the party most immediately slighted, had every reason to condemn Edwardes' supposed pandering to the orders of the Inspector-General and the British Legation. In his interview with Fu, Pratt had taken pains to refute the widely-held belief that Edwardes had acted on British orders. Nevertheless the mud stuck firmly to Edwardes. Whatever the truth of the matter, he had no option but to issue categorical denials of the reports.[34] Moreover, his assertion that he closed the Customs House to "keep it clear of political disturbances" smacked both of a disciplinarian British mentality and of the maintenance of foreign control over Chinese citizens engaged in legitimate protest. Edwardes conspicuously failed to address the issue which concerned the Nationalists, namely that he had refused to take orders from his Superintendent. Questions concerning Edwardes' willingness to submit

---

[32]FO 228/3741/5A/113 1928: Pratt minute of conversation with Fu on 23 July 1928: forwarded to Legation.
[33]Edwardes' reply to his critics was published in the *North-China Standard*, 21 October 1928: enclosed in FO 228/3741/5A/129 1928.
[34]FO 228/3741/5A/113 1928, *q.v.*

to the authority of the Nationalist Government naturally followed.[35] Pratt sensed the symbolic importance of the issue as soon as it was raised and warned that "this may seriously prejudice the chances of [Edwardes'] appointment as I.-G."[36]

Supporting the evidence of this one issue were several indications that Edwardes was not the type of Inspector-General who would adequately meet Nationalist requirements. His refusal to countenance the *pro rata* division of Customs revenue between North and South had created an unfortunate impression of his intentions, despite his later attempts to mollify the nationalists with his proposals on the tariff. After Chang formally dissolved the Peking Shui-wu Ch'u in July 1928, following the Nationalist victory in the Northern Expedition, he found ample evidence of continued *ultra vires* action by Edwardes, including the unauthorised allocation of revenues to ten agencies of the Peking Government. During his tenure in Peking Edwardes was alleged to have provided Chang Tso-lin with 850,000 dollars of Customs revenue with no oversight by the Diplomatic Body.[37] Whether Chang's allegations were in fact of any substance, Edwardes' attitude towards Customs affairs and his close connection with the unquestioned hostility of Aglen to the South were enough to threaten his confirmation and to feed the Shanghai and Nanking rumour-mills. He was in fact upbraided by Lampson over his carelessness in drawing a cheque on the revenue for the sum of 150,000 dollars, payable to the Peking politician Ou Tching and ostensibly to cover the expenses of the Peking defence force. Ou cashed the cheque and promptly fled Peking with the money.[38] Chang's secretary had also leaked to Edwardes' Chinese secretary the information that Chang was planning to reform the service and intended to appoint Maze over Edwardes.[39]

Edwardes was doubtless perplexed by the attacks made upon him. His attitude to the Customs since his appointment in Peking had tended towards a gradual recognition of the demands of the nationalists, although such grudging recognition carried more than a hint of defiance. He had made what he felt to be a bold proposal for the institution of tariff autonomy. On the advice of the Legation he had also abdicated the controversial responsibilities of a loan guarantor bequeathed to him by Aglen. He was therefore inclined to blame the negative reports upon Shanghai-inspired

[35]Chang, *op. cit.*, p. 117.

[36]FO 371/13195/230: F 4028/46/10: Pratt minute of 1 August 1928 to Lampson cable of 19 July detailing allegations.

[37]Chang, *op. cit.*, pp. 127-131: copies of telegrams to Soong reporting on dissolution of Shui-wu Ch'u, June-July 1928.

[38]*KD* f. 104v-105r (1928): Tuesday June 5th 1928.

[39]FO 228/3741/5A/91 1928: Aveling minute of conversation with Edwardes, 6 July 1928.

propaganda which ignored his genuine devotion to the interests of the Service. In doing so he failed to realise either the full weight or the legitimacy of the allegations made against him.

Edwardes' consistently bad press was, however, taken at face value by Pratt:

> We have had many indications recently that Edwardes is not a *persona grata* with the Nationalists and I feel that he himself is very largely to blame. He is determined to carry on the tradition of Aglen instead of going back to the principles of Sir R. Hart and the Chinese will have none of him.

> [There is] a further indication that the Nationalists have decided to appoint Maze and not Edwardes. If Sir M. Lampson supports the latter too insistently he will be heading for a fall.

> The plain fact is that Edwardes is *persona non grata* to the Chinese. He lacks the one thing that is essential for anyone in his position to have, namely, the knack of getting on with the Chinese. On the contrary, he always seems to rub them up the wrong way. In supporting Mr. Edwardes we have unfortunately backed the wrong horse . . . [40]

Pratt's mournful assessment of Edwardes' prospects of confirmation begs the question of Soong's continued support. Why did the Minister of Finance defend such an unsuitable candidate for so long? Substantial documentation of the issue of the Customs as dealt with by the Nanking Government is not accessible: in its absence some reasonable hypotheses are supported by the available evidence.

Soong's support for Edwardes can be seen as a corollary of his attempt to build as wide a base of support as possible outside the Kuomintang's military establishment and its ideological cliques. In Edwardes' case Soong's patronage had several complementary aims. Aware that Edwardes was the preferred nominee of Great Britain, Soong evidently saw a means of cultivating goodwill with a power which had shown interest in cooperating with the Nanking regime. The more of this goodwill Soong

---

[40]FO 371/13194/10: F 3158/36/10: Pratt minute to Legation telegram of 20 June reporting that Chang rumoured to be about to appoint Maze. FO 371/13194/172: F 3260/46/10: Pratt minute to Lampson telegram of 23 June stating that Edwardes was in "apostolic succession." FO 371/13195/279: F 5868/46/10: Pratt minute to Lampson cable of 26 October reporting Edwardes' difficulties with Soong in Shanghai.

could channel through his person, the better for him and the better for the stability of the financial markets and the economy.

Edwardes had also shown an interest in implementing tariff autonomy, an issue which Soong was anxious to remove from the field of partisan rhetoric. If he could achieve an accommodation with a compliant Edwardes, thereby delivering a moderate and economically viable tariff package to the South, his position would be immeasurably strengthened, not only *vis-à-vis* the rest of the government and Party, but also *vis-à-vis* his own commercial constituency. Moreover, the establishment of a close working relationship with the new Inspector-General could wean him from foreign control. If there was one person in Nanking well-equipped to harness Edwardes and to persuade him to shed some of Aglen's more objectionable intellectual baggage, that man was T.V. Soong.

Furthermore, the rhetoric of Customs reform which Chang and Maze were beginning to parade around Shanghai and Nanking must have concerned Soong the pragmatist. The autonomy of the Customs was a fine slogan, but fine slogans did not necessarily inspire confidence within the bond markets upon which Soong relied for his fiscal independence. If a group of ideologues were to take control of the Customs administration and hold it in thrall to the dictates of nationalism, there was no telling how far business confidence in Chinese credit might fall, and thus how difficult it would be to float loan issues with the Revenue as security. Soong was joined in this concern by a small but influential sector of the Chinese banking community. At the head of this group was Chang Kia-ngau, whose associations with Aglen had been transferred to the latter's successor. However, Chang Fu-yun's threat to Soong's authority also grew as the former began to profit from Edwardes' apparent indiscretions, and by August 1928 it must have become clear to Soong that his support for Edwardes had forced him into a highly dangerous political position.

These hypotheses are supported by the available facts. A definitive statement of the mentality of Soong and his attitude to Customs affairs will have to await a more thoroughly-researched political biography. It seems logical, however, to suggest that Soong would have found the Customs question of vital financial importance and would not have been as keen as some of his fellow ministers to make it the flagship of a rights-recovery drive.

Soong's attempts at gaining Edwardes' confidence were largely thwarted by the entrenched position which Maze had occupied at Shanghai. Maze's control over forty per cent of the Customs revenue made him a force to be reckoned with, as did his contacts within the Nanking government. Edwardes was to reiterate that his position as Officiating Inspector-General in Peking was intolerable as long as Maze remained in Shanghai. The

86

machinery which the Kuan-wu Shu developed for the submission of Service moves merely compounded the insult to Edwardes' office and dignity. An initial effort to remove Maze from the arena by waiting until he took his scheduled leave on April 15 foundered when the Shanghai General Chamber of Commerce and the Shanghai Shipping Association, apparently acting independently of the Government, successfully petitioned the Shu to cancel the leave.[41]

Edwardes was shortly afterwards approached by Chang Kia-ngau, acting as Soong's unofficial emissary. Chang apologised for Soong's failure to present a more acceptable formula whereby Service moves could be communicated to Nanking, but begged Edwardes to be patient. Soong, he said, was in a very delicate position as regarded the Kuomintang, and he could not afford to deviate from the party line at this crucial stage in the Northern Expedition lest he come under attack for disloyalty.[42]

In May Chang addressed Edwardes in more peremptory fashion, suggesting that he render specific services to the Nationalists in return for his confirmation. In this blatant *quid pro quo*, Chang envisaged Edwardes' serving as the custodian of a new Sinking Fund, a proposal reminiscent of the practices of Aglen's heyday. In return Edwardes would receive his confirmation. His tone was little short of threatening, and caused some alarm in the Legation when the approach was divulged by Edwardes: Basil Newton found the approach "improper, impertinent and inaccurate," and Frank Aveling had to point out that Chang was an old friend of Edwardes and had not meant to be so provocative.[43] However, the approach was not necessarily out of character, nor utterly unexpected. In July 1927 Chang had approached Maze with a request that he invite E.O. Reis, the manager of the Consolidated Loan Service, to Shanghai for confidential talks over the future of the loans. He also approached Edwardes to ask that the former confirm the security on domestic bonds. Edwardes demurred, as he had given up his responsibilities to the domestic loan service on the advice of the Legation. Chang persisted, however, and it appears that he eventually persuaded Edwardes to supervise a formal registration of the bonds. Whatever comprised the legal fictions which underlay such an arrangement, it was clear that the Acting Inspector-General was not inclined to forswear close

---

[41]*MP* Ia/II p. 132: Shanghai General Chamber of Commerce and Shanghai Shipping Association letter to Maze of 11 February 1928: corroborated in Chang, *op. cit.*, p. 118, and FO 228/3740/5A/73 1928, letter from Soong to Edwardes of 21 March 1928.

[42]FO 228/3740/5A/73 1928: letter from Chang Chia-ao (Kia-ngau) to Edwardes of 18 April 1928.

[43]FO 228/3740/5A/77 1928: file notes to Chang Kia-ngau letter to Edwardes of 7 May 1928.

association with the modern Chinese banking communities of Peking and Shanghai.[44]

Once Peking fell to Nationalist forces the threat of a Customs split disappeared. Instead of holding the Service to ransom, Nanking now had to consider how the Service was to be administered as a whole. Chang Fu-yun was eager to implement his plans for reform as soon as possible, and suggested that Soong appoint Maze: "Soong, however, wished to take his time and wait, gave me no reasons, and did not act."[45] Chang went north regardless and gathered information on Edwardes' malfeasance. At a British Legation dinner given for the visiting Vice-Minister of Foreign Affairs from Nanking, Chang found himself seated next to Lampson, who declared his personal and official confidence in Edwardes and refused to sanction Maze. This inflamed Chang's righteous nationalism: "What British auspices there were [over the Customs Service] were encroachments on Chinese administrative authority of British influence. Sir Miles did not want to know what China wanted but what he wanted." Lampson, for his part, had "a suspicion that [Chang was] strongly anti-Edwardes himself."[46]

Lampson continued his vigorous lobbying on Edwardes' behalf, and received a categorical assurance from Soong that the latter had his backing. Soong was, however, worried about the Fifth Party Plenum which was due to convene in early August, and said that he could not move to confirm Edwardes' appointment until he had steered his own financial proposals through. He expected opposition to Edwardes to come from the Kwangsi clique of C.C. Wu, Hu Han-min and Li Chai-sum, and promised to resign if he could not achieve confirmation.[47] With regard to Maze, Soong declared him "unfitted for the post . . . [and] unsuitable for employment in any public service." Lampson had also told Chang Kia-ngau of Maze's disloyalty and had received the assurance that "prominent Chinese bankers" strongly supported Edwardes.[48]

By the summer of 1928 the capitalist coalition which Soong had forged was beginning to outgrow its tutelage. In July the Shanghai General Chamber of Commerce had threatened to refuse to pay the new *likin*

---

[44]*MP* Ia/II, pp. 67-70: letters from Chang to Maze of 18 July 1927 and from Chang to Edwardes of 21 July 1927.

[45]Chang, *op. cit.*, p. 124.

[46]*Ibid.*, pp. 125-26. Lampson's account of the conversation is in *KD*, f. 131v-132r (1928): 17 July 1928.

[47]In fact both Wu and Hu were out of the country at the beginning of August, Wu having taken up the post of Minister to the United States. It is not known whether Hu and the rest of the Kwangsi clique had returned from their European tour in time for the opening of the Plenum on 7 August.

[48]FO 228/3741/5A/93 1928: Lampson wire to F.O. of 18 July 1928 reporting meetings with Soong and Chang.

assessments, while Chapei businessmen were defiantly funding a Merchants Volunteer Corps.[49] This unwelcome independence threatened Soong's fiscal base as well as his political credibility. The outspoken demands of the business community were beginning to be an embarrassment and a liability.

Soong prepared for the Fifth Party Plenum by having the National Economic Conference pass a resolution in favour of Edwardes' retention. It was argued that to remove Edwardes would be to undermine the security of the government bond market. However, press opinion railed against the decision. In what appeared to be a campaign orchestrated as much against Soong as against Edwardes, the latter's offences against Chinese nationalism were fully exposed and duly embellished.[50] The capitalists of the National Economic Conference thus stood accused of putting personal profit before the interests of the nation, and there was even strong pressure for Soong to appoint a Chinese Inspector-General.[51] Although the Plenum passed Soong's plan in early August, creating a National Budget Committee and Central Financial Reorganization Committee, the authority Soong had over the largely military membership of these committees was sharply diminished.

Soong took the press campaign as a warning to proceed cautiously on matters of symbolic national interest. Already under fire for his collusion with capitalist elements to the exclusion of other social classes, he could not risk a charge of betraying the Revolution. Thus when he invited Edwardes to Shanghai at the end of August he asked the latter not to publicise the event. The *North-China Daily News* stated that Edwardes was going South to discuss the raising of extra revenues, as well as to ratify his own position.[52] On 11 September Soong informed Edwardes of his decision to appoint him Officiating Inspector-General for the time being, while investigating ways to send Maze home on leave.[53] By 16 September, however, Soong had backed

---

[49]For this paragraph, Coble, *op. cit.*, pp. 54-58.

[50]The Shanghai Amalgamated Union of Chinese Customs Employees sent an open message to the Government on 30 July, enumerating Edwardes' wrongdoings and demanding that "the Chinese Government should be master in its own house." FO 228/3741/5A/98 1928: Garstin (Acting Consul-General, Shanghai) cable to Lampson of 30 July 1928. The Chinese Chambers of Commerce sent a similar telegram urging the appointment of Maze, which the Legation took as evidence of Maze propaganda. FO 228/3741/5A/99 1928: Barton cable to Lampson of 8 August 1928. The *Shih Shih Hsin Pao* ran an editorial on 3 August demanding the dismissal of Edwardes, "an enemy of the Nationalist Revolution," and hinting at the suitability of Maze: *MP* Ia/II pp. 187-89. The *China Weekly Review* noted the barrage of protest in the Chinese press and published a long editorial to coincide with the Plenum: *CWR* (August 11, 1928), pp. 347-350. For press criticism of the National Economic Committee, see Coble, *op. cit*, p. 58.

[51]Dayer, *Finance and Empire*, p. 271n.

[52]FO 228/3741/5A/102 1928, Lampson wire to F.O. of 23 August 1928: *NCH* (8 September 1928, report of 31 August), p. 394.

[53]FO 228/3741/5A/104 1928: Garstin cable to Lampson of 11 September 1928.

away from the confirmation: he told Edwardes that he needed the approval of Hu Han-min and Chang Ching-chiang, chairman of the Board of Reconstruction, for the appointment. To confirm Edwardes unilaterally would apparently jeopardise Soong's job.[54] He appeared to be under attack by members of the Kwangsi clique in the period of negotiations leading up to the proclamation of the National Government on 10 October.

The delicacy of Soong's position appeared to be borne out in the stiffly correct manner in which he addressed Edwardes in a letter of 18 September. Soong here stated that the appointment was of such importance and the opposition to it so strong that consultation was vital; that the choice of Edwardes as I.-G. was the best for the Service, but other members of the Government were entitled to hold dissenting opinions; that his blocking of Edwardes' nominations for service moves when Edwardes had been in the pay of Peking had been strictly correct; and that he was not prepared to discipline Maze for insubordination on hearsay evidence.[55] In other words, Soong, in the face of factional opposition, was officially distancing himself from his private support for Edwardes. This was a prudent position to take: Chang Kia-ngau was at the same time being threatened with jail, and the Bank of China threatened with closure, as a consequence of Chang's refusal to raise a loan of ten million dollars for Chiang Kai-shek.[56]

Edwardes found himself in desperate need of support. He told Garstin that he needed Soong to re-establish his authority over Maze and the Chinese Customs staff who were "indulging in private and public denunciation of himself as Head of the Service." He was also aware that his invitation to Shanghai had been intended to curtail the fringe factional activities in which Soong accused Maze of indulging: "Maze had allied himself to a political faction inimical to [Soong] as soon as he realised that it was the Minister of Finance's intention to support Edwardes' appointment."[57] From the admittedly sketchy view of Nationalist factional

---

[54]FO 228/3741/5A/105 1928: Garstin cable to Lampson of 16 September 1928, recording conversation with Edwardes. This was forwarded to the Foreign Office, where Pratt noted that the two officials mentioned were sympathetic towards Maze: FO 371/13195/263: F 5130/46/10: Pratt minute of 24 September 1928. A letter from Maze to Chang Ching-chiang of 7 August 1928 on the subject of improving Chinese communications is in MP Ia/II, pp. 190-92. On 19 September Stephenson received a report from Edwardes that Maze had gained a post on the Reconstruction Committee through "intriguing with T.V. Sung's [sic] chief political opponent in the Kwangsi group"[presumably Chang], and stated that Maze's acceptance of this post while still Shanghai Commissioner was in flagrant contravention of service rules. FO 371/13195/277: F 5464/46/10: Mounsey minute of 10 October 1928 to Lampson telegram of 8 October.
[55]FO 228/3741/5A/110 1928, q.v.
[56]Andrea Lee McElderry, "Robber Barons or National Capitalists", p. 58.
[57]FO 228/3741/5A/105 1928, q.v.

politics which has emerged, it would, however, be more accurate to suggest that Maze's political position had been co-opted by a faction which could make good use of his nationalist convictions.

The internal political situation at Nanking appeared to have calmed a little by the last week in September. On the 22nd, Soong offered to confirm Edwardes as Officiating Inspector-General on the condition that no disciplinary action was to be taken against Maze. At the same time he confirmed Edwardes' sole authority over the appointment of Customs Commissioners.[58] It was also reported that "Hu Han-min had declared that he was opposed to Mr. Maze now in view of the propaganda campaign which the latter had conducted."[59] Edwardes was reassured sufficiently to feel able to leave Shanghai before receiving official confirmation of the appointment.

This official announcement of the confirmation, on October 3rd, therefore came as a shock to Edwardes, as it indicated that Soong had been forced to compromise on the appointment without consulting him. Edwardes was appointed Officiating Inspector-General, whereas Maze was appointed Substantive Deputy Inspector-General in addition to retaining his post as Shanghai Commissioner. It was clear that Edwardes regarded the arrangement as highly unsatisfactory and immediately sought the authority to send Maze on home leave:

> The manifest impossibility of acting as officiating Inspector-General with a substantive Second-in-command who will unscrupulously work for the post during any period in which I might function in that acting appointment requires no explanation from me.[60]

Edwardes subsequently demanded either the removal of Maze or his own confirmation in the substantive post, neither of which requests Soong was in a position to fulfil. Chang indicates that Maze had himself been pressured by the British community in Shanghai to stand down in favour of Edwardes, and had declared his intention to do so if Edwardes achieved governmental recognition. The potential political liability of Maze's resignation could not possibly be countenanced. Soong had therefore taken steps to rein Maze in, presumably until such time as he could be effectively dismissed by the Government. Maze's appointment as Deputy Inspector-General was explained by Chang as a safeguard against dismissal by Edwardes, the post being in the gift of the government.[61] Certainly any

[58]FO 228/3741/5A/108 1928: Garstin cable to Lampson of 23 September 1928.

[59]FO 228/3741/5A/110 1928: Lampson minute of conversation with Edwardes, 28 September 1928.

[60]FO 228/3741/5A/121: Edwardes letter to Lampson of 6 October 1928.

[61]Chang, *op. cit.,* p. 132.

action by Edwardes against Maze would have been catastrophic at this juncture, given the latter's popularity in nationalist circles. The symbolism of a British Inspector-General dismissing the most experienced commissioner in the Service for what amounted to sympathy for the nationalist cause would have plunged Soong into a political crisis compared to which his ordeal in September would have appeared idyllic. If Maze was to be dismissed, he would have to be dismissed by the government, and for very clear reasons.

Edwardes patently misread the situation, however, and continued to demand action against Maze. Even Lampson was astute enough to realise that the issue was not to be forced in this fashion, and actively warned Edwardes against making such dangerous demands. His protests were to no avail. Edwardes was by now thoroughly depressed and disillusioned, undoubtedly considered himself out of his depth in nationalist political waters, and saw the issue as one upon which he could usefully make a stand. On 15 November he delivered an ultimatum to Soong: the latter should take action against Maze, or authorise Edwardes to act against him, by 31 December to avoid Edwardes' resignation.[62] Such a request at such short notice was impossible for a weakened Soong to fulfil, and he was therefore forced to let the deadline expire. After a week of fruitless casting around for a more compliant appointee, Soong recommended the substantive appointment of Maze as Inspector-General.

Edwardes had been led out of his depth by Soong, who had his own political and financial agenda to fulfil, and whose confident demeanour belied the fact that he was very much isolated within his own party. Edwardes was to blame Maze for having made his position intolerable: yet Maze's alleged insubordination appears merely to have been the outward symptom of a very deep irritation within the Nationalist body politic. Both men had become proxies in a political battle over the future of the Revolution. It was Edwardes' bad fortune to have been drawn into a situation with which he was unfamiliar and to the premises of which he was hostile. Maze, on the other hand, had been far more astute in his assessment of the fundamental issues at stake, and thus found himself delivered to his ultimate goal by virtue of Edwardes' impatience.

---

[62]FO 228/3741/5A/146 1928: Edwardes letter to Lampson of 15 November 1928.

# 8

# Resignation, Resolution, Retreat

The statement of resignation which Edwardes issued was brief but pointed. It attributed his decision to the development of an intolerable "dual control" in the Customs Service, and implied that Soong had been unwilling or unable to settle the situation to his nominee's satisfaction. Edwardes was thus resigning to maintain "the fine traditions of efficiency and discipline which have characterised the Customs Service during the past seventy years."[1]

The gentlemanly tenor and icy reserve of the statement complemented the message of self-sacrifice which it conveyed. Edwardes was yet another Briton who was to be complimented for having done "the decent thing": "his action, besides being that of a man of personal self-respect and dignity, was in the best interests of the service as a whole."[2] The British press was swift to mourn the personal tragedy of Edwardes' departure, and equally swift to identify a scapegoat. As the *North-China Daily News* pointed out, with some acerbity,

> it would be idle to pretend that Mr. Maze's appointment as Inspector-General of Customs is pleasing either to foreigners or to the most responsible Chinese. We do not suppose that he himself is under any illusions in this respect. The events of the past eight or nine months are too generally known for the circumstances of the appointment to be acceptable.[3]

On the day following Edwardes' resignation the *North China Standard* reported the Peking and Shanghai gossip which surrounded the affair. Maze was alleged to have been motivated by personal ambition in "thrusting" against Edwardes. His demand for British honours denied, he had sought to gratify himself in "close coordination with the Nanking

---

[1] The full text of the statement is reproduced in *CWR* (5 January 1929), p. 1.
[2] *The Week in China* (12 January 1929), p. 42.
[3] *NCDN* (12 January 1929), p. 6.

Ministry of Finance." Edwardes' resignation had amply demonstrated the success of this approach. Maze had not only worked against his superior officer in the Customs: he had also set out to destroy the integrity of the Customs in the face of the Powers themselves.[4]

The natural assumption following the allegations of Maze's intrigue was that the new Inspector-General would be in thrall to the faction responsible for his appointment. "In the highest Chinese banking circles no concealment is being made of the belief that Mr. Maze has been put into office by a particular clique, which in due time will present its bill for payment."[5] Though Press comment was in general sanguine about the prospects for the Customs, many commentaries manifested a residual distrust of Chinese officialdom. Maze's inaugural promise of adaptation and change "in an age of changes" was unlikely to reassure a foreign community which had been used to counting on the Customs Service as the acme of Western bureaucratic propriety.

As the previous chapter has shown, what appeared on the surface to be a tragic tale of greed and intrigue was in fact a far deeper manifestation of a struggle between the ideological and the pragmatic in the Nationalist Government. This should not, however, imply that foreign interest in the case was in effect an irrelevant intrusion into China's internal affairs. The furore over Maze's appointment had laid bare some fundamental assumptions about the role of the foreigner in China, while the example of Maze's service demonstrated the ability of the foreigner to approach a felicitous state of Hartian synarchy.

———————————

The mentality which seventy years earlier had sanctioned the shelling the Taku forts and the sack of the Imperial Summer Palace was dusted off in July 1928. Harry Fox, Commercial Counsellor to the Legation, penned this considered minute on the legitimacy of the Nanking government.

> It seems to me that the real point at issue—leaving on one side the important question of our interest in the integrity of the Customs Loan service—is not should we support Edwardes because he is a better man than Maze—or vice versa, or support neither because there is little to choose between them, but are we going to sit still and let a hardly-fledged Chinese Government to dismiss for purely personal reasons a British subject who has rendered his predecessors loyal

———————————

[4]*North China Standard* (1 January 1929), report by G.W. Gorman: enclosed in FO 228/3943/5A/2 1929.
[5]*NCDN, loc. cit.*

service in a position of great responsibility and has worthily maintained the high tradition set up by the great Englishman who first gave the Chinese their Customs Service? If we allow this to take place we shall encourage the more irresponsible elements in the new Government to deal in similarly cavalier fashion with any foreigners in Chinese Government service who happen to incur their dislike— and soon no foreigner's post in the government service will be worth a month's purchase. It is not only Edwardes' battle we are fighting but the claim of every Englishman & foreigner in China . . . to a square deal in every case that he has deserved it . . . [6]

Lampson appeared to approve these sentiments, for he used much the same language in a telegram to the Foreign Office which inveighed against the unsuitability of Maze and the unsavoury precedent which his success would set for the future employment of foreigners who valued their integrity in the face of Chinese corruption.[7] Yet his diary sets a slightly different tone:

This is a pretty kettle of fish, and I really don't know where we are; in fact, I feel very strongly on the whole question, for through the supineness of the people at home, as I hold at least, I have been placed in a thoroughly ridiculous and degrading position, and I don't quite know what I should do. But to sit still and do nothing is a little difficult: one's self-respect demands that one should do something, but what! It is no good asking for a transfer, because that would not help.[8]

In the expression of these views it is possible to see the spirit of the December Memorandum strained to breaking-point. Although the South had claimed the military unification of China, the form of government in Nanking had still not taken on any reasonable definition. Britain was still waiting for a settlement of the Nanking Incident before recognition of the regime could be considered. That same regime was now claiming the right to decide the fitness of a British subject, in whom the Legation had placed its confidence, to take up a post in its civil service. Bitten once in the case of Aglen, the Legation was hardly prepared to stand by while another Briton received an insult to his character, integrity, honour and abilities. Yet in the present political climate such a view was not enforceable save by the imposition of sanctions on the Nationalists. Given that the December Memorandum had specifically exhorted the Powers not to take so rigid a

---

[6]FO 228/3741/5A/91 1928: Fox file note of 6 July 1928. One assumes that by "the great Englishman" Fox means the Ulsterman Robert Hart.
[7]FO 228/3741/5A/91 1928: Lampson wire to F.O. of 9 July 1928.
[8]*KD*, f. 2v (1929): 9 January 1929.

stance on the invocation of every treaty right, it would now be difficult for Britain to take such a stance on an appointment over which she had no control enforceable by treaty.[9] All that existed to demonstrate any British right whatsoever was the Tsungli Yamen note of 1898, which did little more than establish the presumption of British approval of the appointment of an Inspector-General of Customs.

The structure of informal empire had nevertheless been built upon such presumptions, and however much they may have seemed ripe for removal, they represented the sole security available to the foreigner in China. Yet it was only through trading on this security that the Foreign Office could demonstrate that it was serious in its policy of conciliation. Austen Chamberlain had told Lampson as soon as July 1928 that "though there are obvious objections to Maze, yet he has ability and sound judgment and [the] Chinese might well make a much worse selection."[10]

The Foreign Office had gradually come to realise that Edwardes was the candidate of default. He had been selected, as Lampson had put it, by "apostolic succession" when Aglen was dismissed; there were no apparent alternatives to his nomination; and he had apparently survived his first year as Acting Inspector-General through a reliance on the Legation which none of his predecessors had dared to show.[11] Nevertheless, during his tenure as Officiating I.-G. he had apparently done nothing untoward and had seemed quite prepared to maintain the British interest in a stable and unified Customs Service. When the question of his confirmation arose in January 1928, the Foreign Office had backed him as "the most suitable candidate" for the post, given that there was little to be said against him and the fringe benefits of his confirmation (long tenure and the support of the Japanese) were attractive. When Maze subsequently displayed his lack of patriotic qualities, Edwardes gained further support, much of it from the fact that he was apparently the hapless victim of an unfair intrigue.

Yet once it became clear that Edwardes would face stern opposition in the South, his candidature began to be reassessed in Whitehall. The threats of the South and the apparent intrigues of Maze had galvanised Lampson into fighting for Edwardes' confirmation, partly for fear of otherwise appearing weak, foolish or perfidious. The Foreign Office, however, found itself under no such constraints. Once it had become apparent that Edwardes' standing had been seriously damaged by his past insensitivity to nationalist sentiment, the cost of forcing his candidature upon

---

[9]FO 371/13195/272: F 5380/46/10: Mounsey minute of 5 October 1928 to Lampson telegram of 4 October.

[10]FO 228/3741/5A/89 1928: wire from Chamberlain to Lampson of 3 July 1928.

[11]See above, p.apostolic succession84n.

Nanking appeared to be too high. The experiences of the anti-foreign movement had taught the Foreign Office that it was futile to attempt to debate the facts of issues whose symbolic value had grown far beyond their original significance. To demand that Nanking appoint Edwardes would merely confirm the allegations of British control which Edwardes was doing his utmost to deny.

It was clear, furthermore, that in Customs policy Edwardes was developing the high-handed attitude towards Chinese aspirations which had been characteristic of the tenure of his predecessor. Pratt noted that

In his remarks about foreign control of revenue Mr. Edwardes shows the cloven hoof, in other words Sir F. Aglen's training. Mr. Edwardes never realises that foreign control of the revenue only began in 1912, that it is only reasonable and natural that the Chinese should now wish to reassert control.[12]

The quarrels which the Foreign Office had had with Aglen had gone far beyond his refusal to submit the revenue to Chinese authority. Nevertheless Edwardes was showing a similar inability to regard the nationalist movement with anything other than fear and hostility. It was fast becoming evident that for the Foreign Office to nail Edwardes' colours to the mast and fearlessly to press for his confirmation would be a most misguided and provocative course to take.

From the time that the Legation had realised that it was Maze's very presence in Shanghai which was prejudicial to Edwardes' chances of confirmation, Lampson had tirelessly petitioned the Foreign Office for the authority to take sanctions against Maze. One of the options he had in mind was the use of the so-called "consular clearance" system, whereby the Shanghai consul would relieve the Shanghai Commissioner of the task of clearing Customs duties. The Foreign Office, however, found this method of dealing with the situation inappropriate, and informed Lampson that he was not to use it simply for the purpose of installing Edwardes.[13] Chamberlain himself refused to sanction these "strong measures" and suggested that, should Maze be appointed, Lampson would have to accept the situation with good grace.[14]

The October appointment of Maze as Edwardes' substantive deputy increased the threat of Edwardes' resignation should the South not respond to diplomacy or pressure. Lampson made his views quite clear: "I should like to emphasise that if Edwardes goes it will be quite impossible for me to

---

[12]FO 371/13195/288: F 6811/46/10: Pratt minute to Garstin cable of 12 December 1928.
[13]FO 228/3741/5A/89 1928: Chamberlain wire to Lampson of 3 July 1928, q.v.
[14]FO 228/3741/5A/94 1928: Chamberlain wire to Lampson of 21 July 1928.

work with Maze."[15] The junior minister Lord Cushendun felt obliged to remind Lampson that his support for Edwardes, who had taken an "injudicious course" in demanding Maze's removal, should not be allowed to jeopardise other continuing negotiations with the Nanking Government regarding official recognition and the ratification of a tariff treaty. If Maze was appointed Edwardes would be partly to blame for having forced the issue: the situation would be "unfortunate and difficult" but would have to be accepted.[16]

Lampson now found himself caught between duty, conscience and inclination. Despite Lampson's entreaties, Edwardes would not be dissuaded from forcing the issue, and again threatened to resign. Lampson could not countenance the departure of Edwardes, neither could he satisfy him that a policy of waiting for Maze's dismissal by the government would have any effect or stem Maze's capacities for further intrigue in Shanghai. The January promises of Foreign Office support for Edwardes as "the candidate best qualified" for the post of Inspector-General now appeared to have no weight whatsoever in the absence of forceful sanctions.[17] Edwardes was profoundly disillusioned with the Far Eastern Department, which he described as "Pratt and his committee of arbiters of British national policy," and predicted that it would use any false moves on his part to justify a lack of active support.[18]

Stymied in its attempts to gain official Foreign Office support for Edwardes or sanctions against Maze, the Legation turned to the commercial community in the hope that it might bring more pressure to bear. There is circumstantial evidence to suggest that Garstin, the Acting Consul-General at Shanghai, connived at the release of information deliberately aimed at discrediting Maze. In a confidential cable to Lampson in early November he expressed the opinion that "Maze's position here is likely to become increasingly disagreeable as [the] foreign community are beginning to realise the part that he has been playing." Garstin also suggested that the Government might indicate to Maze that he should leave Shanghai, "but in view of [the] attitude of Maze last February I am doubtful whether this will be a good move."[19] In November, G. Hussey-Freke, the head of the Salt

[15]FO 228/3741/5A/114 1928: Lampson telegram to F.O. of 4 October 1928.
[16]FO 228/3741/5A/116 1928: Cushendun cable to Lampson of 5 October 1928.
[17]FO 228/3741/5A/119 1928: Lampson record of telephone conversation with Edwardes, 5 October 1928.
[18]FO 228/3741/5A/145 1928: letter from Edwardes to Aveling of 15 November 1928.
[19]FO 228/3741/5A/135 1928: cable from Garstin to Lampson of 2 November 1928. On January 4th Lampson noted on the file of the *North China Standard* report of Maze's request for a decoration: "Personally I regret this indiscretion, which gives (almost literally) Maze's request . . . I must know where this indiscretion occurred . . . it is a great pity, & the F.O. may

Revenue Administration, had told Lampson that Maze's name "was now mud in Shanghai. He [Hussey-Freke] had not heard a good word said of him."[20] When Lampson visited Shanghai in December, he found "the whole British Mercantile Community solid on the question" of Maze: the British Chamber of Commerce was encouraging its associates in London and Manchester to lobby the Government in defence of the integrity of the Customs.[21] These protests, however, arrived at the Foreign Office too late to save Edwardes, who by that time had submitted his final ultimatum and was not expecting a positive response.

By the third week of December, therefore, Lampson and Chamberlain had locked horns in what proved to be a purely academic debate over the question of the use of force. Chamberlain had stated that to declare Maze *persona non grata* would give the Nationalists every incentive to appoint him and openly flout British authority. No longer could Britain compel the Chinese to respect her wishes. Maze was, moreover, a servant of the Chinese Government, and British objections to him were solely based upon this service: to declare the official of a foreign government *persona non grata* in connection with the performance of his duties for that government would surely be considered unwarrantable interference in the internal affairs of China.

Lampson countered with a different diplomatic vision. He had hoped that the Nationalists would not want to impair the further development of good relations by going against the express wishes of the British and Japanese Governments, both of which had pledged their support to Edwardes. His last flourish, however, had less to do with diplomacy and more to do with the historical role of the British in China:

> It is difficult out here in China to realise that H.M. Government are prepared to acquiesce without some form of protest in the appontment of such a man [Maze] to control the Customs, maintenance of integrity and honest administration of which has for so long been one of the fundamentals of British policy in China. His appointment will set a premium on disloyalty, intrigue for personal gain and incursion

---

very well ask us how it occurred. So far as I know it wasn't here in Peking." Lampson ordered that the report not be sent to the Foreign Office. FO 228/3943/5A/2 1929.

[20]*KD*, f. 195r (1928): 8 November 1928.

[21]FO 228/3741/5A/152 1928: cable from Lampson (Shanghai) to Legation of 15 December 1928, copied to F.O.

into Chinese domestic politics which has happily been rare in the Customs Service in the past.[22]

The authors of the December Memorandum stuck by their principles regardless. The Foreign Office's refusal to involve itself in the Maze-Edwardes controversy indicated that the time had come to stay out of Chinese administrative matters. Whether dictated by principle or by the pragmatic judgment that to antagonise the Nationalists would again jeopardise British trade, the decision asserted the principle that the 'man on the spot' was not always correct when it came to matters of Chinese national interest. The outcome of the case had disheartened the Legation and incensed many Britons in China, but its effect was to give a considerable jolt to the structure of informal empire. The Inspector-General of Customs now submitted to Chinese control, and, although British, could not be considered the pillar of the foreign community which his predecessors had been. He called for change in the Customs administration. In the eyes of many Britons he had already achieved rather too much.

The circumstances of Maze's inauguration as Inspector-General were inauspicious. Before taking the oath of office he bowed to the portrait of Sun Yat-sen and joined in the recitation of a copy of his will: then, as legally required of all servants of the Nationalist Government, he promised, in Chinese, to "obey the will of the President and accept the principles of the Kuomintang," as well as "to submit to punishment of the severest kind which shall be imposed by the Kuomintang."[23] This apparent genuflection to the will of what some still considered a political faction gave rise to a storm of protest in the British press, although Maze was later to point out that Press reports gave a literal translation of what was a highly idiomatic declaration of service. The staunchest defender of extraterritoriality in the English-language press, H.G.W. Woodhead, gave vent to his opinions in an editorial in the Peking and Tientsin Times, stating that Maze had compromised both his nationality and the status of his position.[24]

Maze gave a strong indication as to the future character of his Inspectorate in a blistering manifesto of rebuttal circulated to those papers which had given the inauguration a hostile reception. While he pointed out that there was "nothing derogatory and nothing unreasonable in officially

---

[22]FO 228/3741/5A/154 1928: cable from Chamberlain to Lampson of 17 December 1928 and Lampson's reply of 26 December. FO 228/3943/5A/4 1929: cable from Chamberlain to Lampson of 2 January 1929.
[23]NCDN (11 January 1927), p. 13.
[24]"A Good Mouth-Filling Oath!", Peking and Tientsin Times, 18 January 1929: enclosed in FO 228/3943/5A/12 1929.

stating that I will be true to the Government whose pay I draw," he also set out the difficulties of his position:

> We must, therefore, either bend or break: it is fantastic to suppose that we, alone, can achieve the impossible—the most we can attempt to do is put the brake on drastic change and endeavour, as far as possible, to protect foreign trade, shipping and financial interests. But what we cannot do these days is to administer the Customs in a sort of water-tight compartment independently of the Government and in defiance of Chinese public opinion. I believe that Sir Austen Chamberlain's China policy is the only safe policy that will stand the test of time; but it follows, of course, that a policy of conciliation naturally leads both the Chinese Government and Chinese people to insist that China must exert a stronger and closer control over the Chinese Customs—and this does not lighten the Inspector-General's task![25]

Maze was, therefore, not intent on selling his soul to the Nationalists, although he had some sharp words for the "arrogance" of those who dictated to the governments of which they were officially servants. Having recorded his distaste for Aglen's policies and approach to Customs affairs, he proceeded to open contacts not with the Legation but with the Foreign Office *via* the Non-Resident Secretary. Evidently informed by Chang and others of Lampson's opposition to him, he was also in all probability aware that the scathing report published in the *North China Standard* on the day after Edwardes' resignation had had its origins in the Legation.[26] Thus he made it clear to the Far Eastern Department that his position was a difficult one and that he expected all possible support from British representatives in China.[27]

Although Wellesley and Chamberlain did not approve of Maze's approach, finding that it "savour[ed] a little of the wish to exploit a diplomatic victory," the Legation was nevertheless informed of the absolute necessity of staying on good terms with the Inspectorate-General. It was feared that Maze might otherwise either choose to use his authority in a manner inimical to British interests, or to resign abruptly, leaving the field open for a Chinese successor.[28] Lampson was appalled and undoubtedly embarrassed by this implicit rebuke, but nevertheless replied that he would be "strictly correct" in his dealings with Maze. The hostility between the two

---

[25]*MP* Ia/III, pp. 1-8: Maze memorandum of 10 January 1929.

[26]See above, p.93.

[27]FO 371//13905/1: F 208/52/10: Maze telegram to F.O. *via* Stephenson of 11 January 1929.

[28]FO 228/3943/5A/10 1929: Chamberlain cable to Lampson of 14 January 1929; FO 371/13905/147: F 3068/52/10: Wellesley minute of conversation with Stephenson concerning Maze's difficulties with the Legation, 5 June 1929.

men continued throughout the summer of 1929, as Maze continued to use unofficial channels to complain of Legation hostility. Lampson had met him on an official basis in May and at that time had chosen to admonish him on the improper approaches he had made to the Foreign Office: he also observed that "never in [his] career had [he] to handle such an unpleasant and degrading affair."[29] The Foreign Office endeavoured to improve relations between the two men: Sir Ronald Lindsay addressed a personal letter to Lampson encouraging him to cultivate Maze a little more. Lampson replied that Maze's allegations were groundless and the manner in which he made them irritating. Maze was unpleasant at the best of times and had become a social outcast in Shanghai, for which he probably, and in Lampson's view unjustly, blamed the Legation. Were Maze resident in Peking he would naturally be integrated into the social circle of the Legation, but it would be counterproductive to attempt to force him on the foreign community of Shanghai. Lindsay again urged Lampson to make a "fresh start" with Maze which went beyond mere "correctness," but drew a terse response. It was clear that Maze was going to have to work hard to win the support of the British establishment in China.[30]

He had, however, managed to re-establish his relationship with the Foreign Office. On receipt of one particular account of Maze's intrigues, Pratt had commented "Maze's conduct as here depicted is . . . so idiotic that I should like to hear his side of the story before forming a judgment."[31] That side came forth with a vengeance, as Maze had, naturally, sent a copy of his broadside to the Far Eastern Department. Troubled by its revelations, and wanting to know whether Maze invoked the December Memorandum out of belief or expediency, Mounsey, via Stephenson, invited Maze to give his account of the controversy, and then interviewed Stephenson in an attempt to obtain an objective viewpoint. The minutes which follow indicate something of a Damascene conversion, as for the first time the facts of Maze's background and attitude were juxtaposed with the information on the situation which the Foreign Office had received from Peking. It was concluded that Maze, while not necessarily a pleasant character, had had his position as unfairly undermined as Edwardes'; that Maze had shown a hitherto unrecognised commitment to the nature of the Customs service; and

[29]FO 228/4094/105B/59 1929: Lampson minute of interview with Maze of 21 May 1929. Lampson's diary entry merely notes that he was "rather amused by [Maze's] embarrassed manner." *KD*, f. 37v (1929): 21 May 1929.

[30]The Lindsay correspondence is in FO 228/3943/5A/38 1929: Lindsay to Lampson of 10 July; Lampson to Lindsay of 14 August; Lindsay to Lampson of 16 July (5A/40); Lampson to Lindsay of 2 September.

[31]FO 371/13905/25: F 450/52/10: Pratt minute of 25 January 1929 to copy of letter from Edwardes to Lampson of 25 November 1928.

that Maze was, in terms of intellect and character, the man best equipped to lead the Customs into the Nationalist era. Wellesley's detailed assessment of the situation was quite magisterial and utterly persuasive. In reconstructing two years of accusation and counter-accusation he was able to maintain the consistent theme of Maze's opposition to the loans policy of Aglen, while developing the breadth of vision to explain Maze's resentment at his treatment under the latter's direction. Moreover he accused the Legation of misleading the Foreign Office as to Maze's abilities and his strength of character, even managing to explain away the demand for a decoration as a "not unreasonable" request in the circumstances. As the stock of Maze rose, and as Wellesley claimed to find "not one shred" of substantive evidence against him, so that of Edwardes dropped. The latter now stood accused of having utterly misconceived Customs policy and having stifled the free exchange of ideas within the Service. Maze, on the other hand, had survived "persecution" and was justified in attempting to demonstrate his enemies wrong. Wellesley summed up his minute with a deft approbation:

> A little while ago I went so far as to say in a minute that I should not be surprised if Mr. Maze turned out to be a good Inspector-General in spite of all. I should now be disposed to say that I should be greatly surprised if he did not.[32]

Having despatched his critics and won a measure of Foreign Office support, Maze undertook the task of transforming the Customs into a national Chinese institution with flair and diligence. He was to justify many of his reforms by his study of Hart, consistently adapting Hart's principles of action to contemporary situations. Hard, honest work and the consistent delivery of surprisingly good results did more than anything else to rehabilitate Maze's reputation.

Throughout 1929 the Foreign Office continued to receive encouraging reports of the stable development of the Customs under Maze's stewardship. Maze had acted promptly to quell potential Service dissension in January by issuing a circular which stated that the Kuan-wu Shu did not intend to disrupt the work of the Customs, and that there was no threat either to the position of foreign employees or to their pensions.[33] He was indirectly rewarded with a statement of loyalty from the staff of the Inspectorate, many of whom had served under the Aglen and Edwardes regimes. His reluctance

---

[32]FO 371/13905/37-57: F 911/52/10: minutes by Pratt (22 February 1929), Mounsey (22 February) and Wellesley (11 March) to record of Mounsey interview with Stephenson of 18 February 1929.

[33]MP Ia/III p. 32: copy of Inspector-General's Circular No. 3846, 2nd. series, of 21 January 1929.

to take "petty revenge" on this section of the staff, he said, incurred him the respect of the Chinese banking community, which had apparently feared a purge.[34]

Maze's administration did not cause the immense drop in bond values which had been feared on Edwardes' resignation, and the introduction of China's first autonomous tariff on February 1st had little negative effect on the revenue. Chang Fu-yun recalled that "China's foreign trade and customs revenue rose by leaps and bounds, and there were no grievances from the merchants, Chinese as well as foreign."[35] The Foreign Office was so impressed with the apparent stability of the revenue that in the autumn of 1929 it commissioned a consular survey of business attitudes towards changes in the Customs administration in the major treaty ports. The Legation was less impressed, and saw it as an attempt by Pratt to gloat over an ignoble victory. The reports generated ranged from the enthusiastic to the grudging, and none had serious complaints with the functioning of the Service. George Moss in Canton noted the increased authority of responsible Superintendents and the increased respect in which the Chinese employees held foreign officials.[36] Sir James Jamieson in Tientsin remarked upon the fact that the Inspector-General was less willing to intervene in the case of foreign merchants' grievances than before, while Launcelot Giles in Hankow was aware of a slight decrease in honesty on the part of Chinese officials as well as a large increase in local taxation.[37] Charles Garstin in Shanghai stated that Maze lacked the personal connections with the British mercantile community which Edwardes had enjoyed, and found the administration in general more "servile" to the Chinese Government in failing to defend British traditions. He nevertheless conceded that Chinese grievances within the Service had been substantially met, and that the Service was "not yet a political plaything," thanks in part to the confidence of the business community in the abilities of T.V. Soong.[38]

Maze's greatest symbolic gesture, and the one which caused the most apprehension, was his acquiescence in the decision of the Kuan-wu Shu to end the practice of recruiting foreigners to the Service except in cases of proven specialist ability. This he complemented in May with the issue of a memorandum detailing the conditions and reasons for the promotion of qualified Chinese to responsible positions in the Outdoor Staff. This document was a remarkably reasoned expression of a policy of retreat.

---

[34]*MP* Ia/XIX p. 124: letter from Secretaries of Customs to Maze of 15 February 1929.
[35]Chang, *Memoir*, p. 139.
[36]FO 228/3943/5A/42 1929: despatch from Moss (Canton) to Legation of 5 October 1929.
[37]FO 228/3943/5A/44 1929: Jameson (Tientsin) despatch of 19 October; FO 228/3943/5A/45 1929: Giles (Hankow) despatch of 14 October.
[38]FO 228/3943/5A/46 1929: Garstin (Shanghai) despatch of 22 October.

Taking as his guiding principle the undeniable right of the Chinese to a greater representation in the higher echelons of the Service, Maze went on to elaborate a variety of safeguards which in present circumstances should be established to maintain confidence in the administration. While he declared himself against the immediate promotion of Chinese to commissionerships, citing as his reason the possibility of military coercion without foreign protection, he nevertheless treated his Chinese employees as competent equals. "The fact that Chinese employees know that they are eligible for such posts, and are not being discriminated against merely because they are Chinese, will in itself improve the *moral* [sic] of the service and thus increase its efficiency."[39] There was no insinuation of "moral flabbiness" on the part of the Chinese staff, nor any suggestion that anything other than forcible coercion might lead them to deviate from their duty to the service. Through this demonstration of moderate policy, Maze impressed foreign businessmen and Nationalist officials with his ability to broker a compromise which conceded to each side what it valued the most: continued foreign control of the service, but with the reassurance of the full equality of the Chinese within it.

Lampson was gracious enough to recognise that the Customs administration was functioning far more smoothly under Maze than he had predicted, though he could not resist pointing out Maze's advantageous position in serving a unified Chinese government.[40] He nevertheless retained an "instinctive moral reserve owing to the corruption and inefficiency of most purely Chinese-run governments," and it was only on the conclusion of his China service in 1933 that he showed a full appreciation of Maze's capabilities:

> It must . . . be recognised that Sir Frederick Maze has done as well, and perhaps better, than could have been expected in very difficult circumstances, including the adjustment of the conditions of the Service to the new outlook involved in the policy of His Majesty's Government that the future of China can no longer be developed under foreign tutelage. . . . It must be admitted that Sir Frederick Maze has been notably successful . . . in preserving in these circumstances the prestige and authority of the foreign element in the Service and in maintaining its traditional efficiency.[41]

---

[39] Inspector-General's confidential memorandum of 30 May 1929, enclosed in FO 228/3943/5A/34 1929.

[40] *Ibid.*, covering letter from Lampson to Henderson (Secretary of State) of 15 July 1929.

[41] *DBFP* 2nd. ser. vol. XI, pp. 383-84: "Sir Miles Lampson's review of events in China, 1926–1933." Crown Copyright: reprinted by permission of the Controller of Her Majesty's Stationery Office.

Maze's vindication was complete, even down to the K.C.M.G. he received in 1931 for "services in the British interest." He had succeeded in convincing the Nationalist government of his desire to effect equitable change in the Customs Service, but had nevertheless conceded nothing in the sphere of efficient administration and honest treatment of foreign traders. In returning to the principles which had guided Sir Robert Hart in his service of China, Maze removed prejudice and fear from both sides in the Customs dispute. He had not been the dupe of the Chinese, nor had he sold out to factional interests. In promising fairness he was obliged to maintain a degree of foreign control over the administration, but his efficiency in this respect was such that his *bona fides* could no longer be doubted.

# 9
# The Future of Informal Empire

The case of Frederick Maze demonstrates that it was in fact possible for British officials to come to some accommodation with Chinese demands for sovereign status without making significant concessions on issues which most directly affected British trade. Nevertheless, it would be foolish to consider that Maze's success represented anything other than a short-term victory, however significant. The continued existence of extraterritoriality served if nothing else as a reminder that Maze could never serve the Chinese nation as fully as he would apparently have liked, although in the event his period of service lasted fourteen years, ending in his internment by the Japanese.[1] In his perceptions and his capabilities Maze had demonstrated an uncommon capacity for cooperation with the Chinese, an ability which any successor would find difficult to match.

What is more remarkable for the purposes of this study is the victory it shows for the principles of the December Memorandum, which, after a barren beginning, began to bear fruit once the Legation came to some understanding about the viability of using force in China to impose Britain's will. 'Gunboat diplomacy', with or without gunboats, was swiftly yielding to the gentler arts of cooperation and understanding. It is difficult to conclude that the prejudices which underlay the motivations of Legation officials were ever really swept away. No matter how cordial his relations with individual members of the Nanking cabinets may have been, Lampson's official correspondence tended to view the Nationalist regime as a government under international supervision. His enthusiasm for the abstract principles of the December Memorandum seemed more difficult to maintain once the Kuomintang had begun to test these principles to the limit. He was, however, sustained by the active interest the Foreign Office was taking in Chinese

---

[1]For a survey of Maze's later career, see Nicholas R. Clifford, "Sir Frederick Maze and the Chinese Maritime Customs, 1937–1941", *Journal of Modern History* vol. 37 no. 1 (March 1965), pp. 18-34.

affairs and the confidence which Pratt had in the innate capacity for self-determination of the Chinese people.

Edwardes had left China in February 1929, the question of his pension unsettled: further researches revealed that he had illegally put aside Customs money in a private pension fund, and his attempts to receive some compensation for his travails in the service of King and Country were to no avail. In 1931, therefore, he chose a new country, offering his services to the Japanese as an adviser to the puppet state of Manchukuo, and thereafter peddled such blatant misinformation and innuendo between Britain and Japan as to make one doubt that his allegations against Maze could ever have been believed in the first place.[2]

Maze himself enjoyed the luxury of the vindication of his principles, though to many his actions still seemed suspect if judged against English public-school codes of honour. His behaviour was initially not easily forgiven in Shanghai, where he was asked to resign from the Bowling Club, according to Harry Fox "one of the oldest and possibly the most exclusive British club in Shanghai."[3] When Malcolm MacDonald, son of the British Prime Minister, visited China at the end of 1929, Maze invited him to be his guest, but Lampson advised against it, lest it "prove embarrassing to him (MacDonald) vis-à-vis the community," which "had more or less banned Maze."[4] Warren Swire believed that Maze had behaved "like a dirty dog, in order to become I.G.:" however, his opinion was that there was little to be gained by gratuitously snubbing Maze. He was thankful that two of Swire's key managers had been out of Shanghai when the story broke and thus had not been obliged to shun Maze, and noted that "most of those, who had cut Maze, were rather in a quandary and wishful to get on terms with him again."[5] Jock Swire subsequently hailed Maze's gifts for compromise in his negotiations for a commercial treaty between Hong Kong and Nanking.[6]

Maze had outwitted the Marlburian Aglen, the Etonian Lampson and the Haileburian Edwardes through having stuck to his guns, refusing to defer to concepts of honour and authority which had little meaning to a man

---

[2] Endicott, *Diplomacy and Enterprise*, p. 74n: Trotter, "Backstage Diplomacy", pp. 39-40.

[3] FO 228/3943/5A/38 1929: Fox filenote to Lindsay-Lampson correpondence, 25 August 1929.

[4] *KD*, f. 117r-v (1929): 16 November 1929. Lampson was, however, "careful to point out that I did not wish [MacDonald] to think that I had any bias against Maze personally. The Maze-Edwardes question . . . was past and done with, I hoped."

[5] *JSSP* vol. 51 ("Local Sundries") p. 1185: letter from G.W. Swire to Bernard (Matheson & Co.) of 23 January 1930.

[6] *JSSP* add. 15: letter from J.K. S[wire] (Shanghai) to J[ohn] S[wire] & S[ons] (London) of 26 May 1930. For the treaty, see N. Miners, *Hong Kong under Imperial Rule, 1912–1941* (Hong Kong: Oxford University Press, 1987), pp. 21-22: the agreement was eventually blocked by the Kwangtung provincial lobby in Nanking.

pledged to the service of China. Whether or not he was guilty of intrigue was a question addressed by Wellesley in his comprehensive minute on the case:

> But then again what is intrigue? There is the positive, the suggestive and the passive method. The first is the method of the neophyte, while the second and the third are for more advanced and subtler minds. But only he can claim to be a consummate artist who understands the interplay of all three as the occasion desires. The very essence of success in intrigue is that the methods should be undiscoverable. I cannot believe that anyone of Mr. Maze's mental calibre would be so clumsy as to have recourse to that kind of open intrigue of which he stands accused by the Legation. Precisely because in his case there is nothing concrete to lay hold of I rather suspect him of being a master in the 'ars celare artem' of the subtler methods . . . Mr. Maze remained passive and silent while his opponent became more and more entangled in his own coils. . . . One may call this intrigue if one likes but there is certainly nothing in it to justify the unmeasured vituperation contained in the Peking telegrams or at which we can reasonably take exception; and I am not at all sure that having regard to the circumstances of the case such consummate artistry should not be dignified by the name of diplomacy rather than intrigue. Indeed the only flaw that I can find is that if he did intrigue he should have allowed it to be even suspected at all.[7]

Such acknowledgment, coming from a master practitioner, perhaps did not provide a full absolution of Maze's character but nevertheless dignified his actions. Maze himself left little to chance: his papers were organised, classified, annotated and eventually deposited with the School of Oriental and African Studies at the University of London. The young John King Fairbank, on meeting with Maze on a visit to China in 1932, was made well aware of the Inspector-General's views on the future of the Service, so firmly so that he believed Maze to be "obviously politically motivated."[8]

Maze's achievement, considerable though it was, must nevertheless be seen in the context of the precipitate developments on the Chinese political scene. Maze ably facilitated the transition between a decaying system of informal empire and its replacement by a sovereign Chinese nation largely because his ties to his own nation were weak and his confidence in China was strong. He could show others the way to come to an accommodation with Chinese nationalism, but he could not perpetuate a

---

[7] FO 371/13905/51-52: F 911/52/10: Wellesley minute of 11 March 1929.
[8] John King Fairbank, *Chinabound: A Fifty-Year Memoir* (New York: Harper & Row, 1982), p. 63.

system which by its very nature was antithetical to the spirit of Chinese sovereignty. Moreover, Maze's apparent soundness in matters of race may still have been relative. He eschewed the 'diehard' view which held the Chinese to be lazy and decadent—yet it is difficult to say how he might have dealt with full racial equality in the Service and in private life, and how far he could have lifted the still-heavy burden of foreign expectations from the shoulders of the fledgling Republic.

Although Maze was remarkable for his ability to communicate effectively with the Nationalists, the revival of synarchic cooperation under his inspectorate was ultimately short-lived. Curtailed by the political and military crises which followed the Japanese invasions of 1932 and 1937, any 'new synarchy' could only be transitory. Where Hart had initially failed, Maze aimed to succeed in the gradual elimination of the foreign element from the Customs Service. Had events not overtaken him, he might have remained in Shanghai to see the elimination carried out according to his plan. Given the difficulties inherent in defending and sustaining a foreign presence in China in the age of nationalism, it was Maze's achievement to have shown the foreign establishment how to retreat with grace and honour.

# Bibliography

Unpublished material:

*i) Documentary sources in library collections*

The University of California, Berkeley:

> Chang Fu-yun, "Reformer of the Chinese Maritime Customs", an oral history conducted 1976, 1979 and 1983 by Blaine C. Gaustad and Rhoda Chang, Regional Oral History Office, The Bancroft Library.

Columbia University Library:

> Columbia University Oral History Project: Chang Chia-ao (Chang Kia-ngau), *Autobiography*; depositions by K.P. Chen, Huang Shen Yi-yung (Huang Fu), Fu Ping-chang, C.T. Wang.

Cornell University Library:

> V. K. Wellington Koo, *The Wellington Koo Memoir.* New York: Chinese Oral History Project of the East Asian Institute of Columbia University, Part II: Microfilming Corporation of America, 1978.

> *The Papers of Sir Frederick Maze relating to the Chinese Maritime Customs Service.* East Ardsley, Wakefield, West Yorkshire: Microform Ltd., 1984.

*Great Britain. Foreign Office Confidential Print.* FO 405.

London: Public Record Office.

*Embassy and Consular Archives.* FO 228.

*Foreign Office General Correspondence.* FO 371.

Middle East Centre, St. Antony's College, Oxford.

Diaries of Miles Lampson, first Baron Killearn.

University of London: School of Oriental and African Studies.

Papers of John Swire and Sons. Ltd.

Papers relating to the Chinese Imperial Customs. Aglen papers *inter alia.*

Papers of Sir John Pratt.

## ii) Unpublished dissertations

Aitcheson, Jean. *The Chinese Maritime Customs Service in the Transition from the Ch'ing to the Nationalist Era: An Examination of the Relationship between a Western-style Fiscal Institution and Chinese Government in the Period before the Manchurian Incident.* Ph.D., Modern History: London, School of Oriental and African Studies, 1983.

Bowie, Christopher John. *Great Britain and the Use of Force in China 1919–1931.* D.Phil., Modern History: Oxford, 1983.

Byrne, Eugene. *The Dismissal of Sir Francis Aglen.* B.A., Modern Languages: University of Westminster, 1993.

113

Clark, Peter Gaffney. *Britain and the Chinese Revolution, 1925–1927.* Ph.D., History: University of California, Berkeley, 1973.

Huskey, Charles Layton. *Americans in Shanghai: Community Formation and Response to Revolution, 1919–1928.* Ph.D., History: North Carolina, 1985.

Megginson, William James III. *Britain's Response to Chinese Nationalism, 1925–1927: The Foreign Office Search for a New Policy.* Ph.D., History: George Washington, 1973.

Thomas, Yuen-nui Pauline. *The Foreign Office and the Business Lobby: British Official and Comercial Attitudes to Treaty Revision in China, 1925–1930.* Ph.D., History: London School of Economics and Political Science, 1981.

Wilson, David Clive. *Britain and the Kuomintang, 1924–1928: A Study of the Interaction of Official Policies and Perceptions in Britain and China.* Ph.D., Arts: London, School of Oriental and African Studies, 1973.

Published material:

*i) Newspapers and periodicals*

*The China Weekly Review.* Shanghai, 1927–1929.

*The China Year Book.* Shanghai: North-China Daily News and Herald, 1925–1930.

*North-China Daily News.* Shanghai, 1926–1929.

*The North-China Herald and Supreme Court and Consular Gazette.* Shanghai; 1926–1929.


*ii) Secondary works*

Adshead, S.A.M. *The Modernization of the Chinese Salt Administration, 1900–1920.* Cambridge, Mass.: Harvard University Press, 1970.

Aglen, F.A. "China and the Special Tariff Conference." *The Nineteenth Century and After* vol. 96 no. 570 (August 1924), pp. 282-291.

Arnold, Julean. *China: A Commercial and Industrial Handbook.* Washington, D.C. :United States Department of Commerce, 1926.

Atwell, Pamela. *British Mandarins and Chinese Reformers: The British Administration of Weihaiwei (1898–1930) and the Territory's Return to Chinese Rule.* Hong Kong: Oxford University Press, 1985.

Bergère, Marie-Claire. *The Golden Age of the Chinese Bourgeoisie 1911–1937,* tr. Janet Lloyd. Cambridge: Cambridge University Press, 1989.

Bianco, Lucien. *Origins of the Chinese Revolution*, tr. Muriel Hall. Stanford, Calif.: Stanford University Press, 1971.

Blakeslee, George H. "The Foreign Stake in China." *Foreign Affairs* vol. 10 no.1 (October 1931), pp. 81-91.

Boorman, Howard L., and Richard C. Howard, *Biographical Dictionary of Republican China*, 4 vols. New York: Columbia University Press, 1967–1971.

Borg, Dorothy. *American Policy and the Chinese Revolution, 1925–1928.* New York: East Asian Institute, Columbia University; Octagon Books, 1968.

Chamberlain Joseph P. "The Feetham Report in Shanghai." *Foreign Affairs* vol. 10 no. 1 (October 1931), pp. 145-153.

Chan, Lau Kit-Ching. "The Lincheng Incident—A Case Study of British Policy in China between the Washington Conference (1921–22) and the First Nationalist Revolution (1925–28)." *Journal of Oriental Studies* vol. 10 no. 2 (July 1972), pp. 172-186.

_____. *Anglo-Chinese Diplomacy in the Careers of Sir John Jordan and Yüan Shih-kai.* Hong Kong: Hong Kong University Press, 1978.

Chapman, H. Owen. *The Chinese Revolution 1926–27.* London: Constable and Co., 1928.

Ch'en, Jerome, and Nicholas Tarling eds. *Studies in the Social History of China and South-East Asia: Essays in Memory of Victor Purcell.* Cambridge: Cambridge University Press, 1970.

Chiang, Kai-shek. *China's Destiny, and Chinese Economic Theory.* New York: Roy Publishers, 1947.

Clifford, Nicholas R. "Sir Frederick Maze and the Chinese Maritime Customs 1937–1941." *Journal of Modern History* vol. 37 no. 1 (March 1965), pp. 18-34.

_____. *Retreat from China: British Policy in the Far East, 1937–1941.* Seattle, Wash.: University of Washington Press, 1967.

_____. *Shanghai, 1925: Urban Nationalism and the Defense of Foreign Privilege.* Ann Arbor, Mich.: Center for Chinese Studies, The University of Michigan, 1979.

_____. "A Revolution Is Not a Tea Party: The Shanghai Mind(s) Reconsidered." *Pacific Historical Review* vol. 59 no. 4 (November 1990), pp. 501-526.

_____. *Spoilt Children of Empire: Westerners in Shanghai and the Chinese Revolution of the 1920's.* Hanover, N.H.: Middlebury College Press; University Press of New England, 1991.

Coates, P.D. *The China Consuls: British Consular Officers, 1843–1943.* Hong Kong: Oxford University Press, 1988.

Coble, Parks M. *The Shanghai Capitalists and the Nationalist Government, 1927–37* 2nd. ed. Cambridge, Mass.: Council on East Asian Studies, Harvard University; Harvard University Press, 1986.

Cochran, Sherman. *Big Business in China: Sino-Foreign Rivalry in the Cigarette Industry, 1890–1930.* Cambridge, Mass.: Harvard University Press, 1980.

Cohen, Paul A. *Between Tradition and Modernity: Wang Tao and Reform in Late Ch'ing China.* Cambridge, Mass.: Council on East Asian Studies, Harvard University; Harvard University Press, 1987.

_____. *Discovering History in China: American Historical Writing on the Recent Chinese Past.* New York: Columbia University Press, 1984.

Colville, John Rupert. *Man of Valour: The Life of Field-Marshal The Viscount Gort, VC, GCB, DSO, MVO, MC.* London: Collins, 1977

Crowley, James B., ed. *Modern East Asia: Essays in Interpretation.* New York: Harcourt, Brace and World, 1970.

Curtis, Lionel. *The Capital Question of China.* London: Macmillan & Co., 1932.

Darwent, C. E. *Shanghai: A Handbook for Travellers and Residents.* Shanghai: Kelly and Walsh, 1920.

Davenport-Hines, R.P.T., and Geoffrey Jones eds. *British Business in Asia since 1860.* Cambridge: Cambridge University Press, 1989.

117

Dayer, Roberta Allbert. *Bankers and Diplomats in China 1917–1925: The Anglo-American Relationship.* London: Frank Cass, 1981.

_____. *Finance and Empire: Sir Charles Addis, 1861–1945.* New York: St Martin's Press, 1988.

Dean, Britten. "British Informal Empire: The Case of China." *Journal of Commonwealth and Comparative Politics* vol. 14 (1976), pp. 64-81.

*Documents on British Foreign Policy* 2nd. series, ed. W.N. Medlicott, Douglas Dakin, M.E. Lambert. London: Her Majesty's Stationery Office, 1970.

Duus, Peter, Ramon H. Myers and Mark R. Peattie eds. *The Japanese Informal Empire in China, 1895–1937.* Princeton, N.J.: Princeton University Press, 1989.

Eastman, Lloyd E. *The Abortive Revolution: China under Nationalist Rule, 1927–1937.* Cambridge, Mass.: Council on East Asian Studies, Harvard University; Harvard University Press, 1974.

_____. "New Insights into the Nature of the Nationalist Regime." *Republican China* vol. 9 no. 2 (February 1984), pp. 8-19.

Edwards, E.W. *British Diplomacy and Finance in China, 1895–1914.* Oxford: The Clarendon Press, 1987.

Elvin, Mark, and G. William Skinner eds. *The Chinese City Between Two Worlds.* Stanford, Calif.: Stanford University Press, 1974.

Endicott, Stephen Lyon. *Diplomacy and Enterprise: British China Policy 1933–1937.* Vancouver, B.C.: University of British Columbia Press, 1975.

Esherick, Joseph W. *Reform and Revolution in China: The 1911 Revolution in Hunan and Hubei.* Berkeley, Calif.: Center for Chinese Studies of the University of Michigan; University of California Press, 1976.

Etherington, Norman. "Reconsidering Theories of Imperialism." *History and Theory* vol. 21 (1982), pp. 1-36.

118

Fairbank, John K. ed. *Chinese Thought and Institutions.* Chicago, Ill.: The University of Chicago Press, 1957.

_____. *Chinabound: A Fifty-Year Memoir.* New York: Harper & Row, 1982.

Feuerwerker, Albert. *The Foreign Establishment in China in the Early Twentieth Century.* Ann Arbor, Mich.: Center for Chinese Studies, The University of Michigan, 1976.

Fewsmith, Joseph. "Response to Eastman." *Republican China* vol. 9 no. 2 (February 1984), pp. 19-27.

_____. *Party, State and Local Elites in Republican China: Merchant Organisations and Politics in Shanghai, 1890–1930.* Honolulu: University of Hawaii Press, 1985.

Fitzgerald, John. "The Misconceived Revolution: State and Society in China's Nationalist Revolution, 1923–1926." *Journal of Asian Studies* vol. 49 no. 2 (May 1990), pp. 323-343.

*The Foreigner in China: An Outline History of Foreign Relations in China, of the Reasons for China's Descent into Chaos, of the Soviet's Plot in Fostering Confusion, and of the Chinese "Nationalist" Reaction to these Several Influences.* Shanghai: North-China Daily News and Herald, 1927.

Friedman, Edward, and Mark Selden eds. *America's Asia: Dissenting Essays on Asian-American Relations.* New York: Vintage Books, 1971.

Fung, Edmund S.K. *The Diplomacy of Imperial Retreat: Britain's South China Policy, 1924–1931.* Hong Kong: Oxford University Press, 1991.

Gallagher, John, and Ronald Robinson. "The Imperialism of Free Trade." *Economic History Review* 2nd. series, vol. VI no 1 (January 1953), pp. 1-15.

Gannett, Lewis S. *Young China.* New York: The Nation, 1927.

119

Geisert, Bradley. "Probing KMT Rule: Reflection on Eastman's 'New Insights'." *Republican China* vol. 9 no. 2 (February 1984), pp. 28-39.

Gillin, Donald G. *Falsifying China's History: The Case of Sterling Seagrave's The Soong Dynasty*. Stanford, Calif.: Hoover Institution; Stanford University Press, 1986.

Goldman, Merle, ed. *Modern Chinese Literature in the May Fourth Era*. Cambridge, Mass.: Harvard University Press, 1977.

Gull, E.M. *British Economic Interests in the Far East*. New York: Institute of Pacific Relations, 1943.

Hall, R.O. *China and Britain*. London: Church of England Zenana Missionary Society, 1927.

Hart, Sir Robert, *These from the Land of Sinim*. London, 1901.

Henriot, Christian. "Municipal Power and Local Elites." *Republican China* vol. 11 no. 2 (April 1986), pp. 1-21.

Hewlett, Sir Meyrick. *Forty Years in China*. London: Macmillan & Co., 1944.

Hodgkin, Henry T. *Recent Events in China*. London: Friend's Bookshop, for the Committee of the Religious Society of Friends, 1925.

Hook, Elizabeth. *A Guide to the Papers of John Swire and Sons Ltd*. London: School of Oriental and African Studies, 1977.

Howe, Christopher ed. *Shanghai: Revolution and Development in a Chinese Metropolis*. Cambridge: Cambridge University Press, 1981.

Hsiao Liang-lin. *China's Foreign Trade Statistics 1864–1949*. Cambridge, Mass.: East Asian Research Center, Harvard University, 1974.

Huebner, Jon. "Architecture on the Shanghai Bund." *Papers on Far Eastern History* (Australian National University, Department of Far Eastern History) no. 39 (September 1989), pp. 127-165.

Huskey, James Layton. "The Cosmopolitan Connection: Americans and Chinese in Shanghai during the Interwar Years." *Diplomatic History* vol. 11 no. 3 (Summer 1987), pp. 227-243.

*The I.G. In Peking: Letters of Robert Hart, Chinese Maritime Customs 1868–1907* ed. John King Fairbank, Katherine Frost Bruner, Elizabeth MacLeod Matheson. Cambridge, Mass.: The Belknap Press of Harvard University Press, 1975.

Iriye, Akira. *After Imperialism.* Cambridge, Mass.: Harvard University Press, 1965.

Israel, John. *Student Nationalism in China 1927–37.* Stanford, Calif.: Hoover Institution on War, Revolution and Peace; Stanford University Press, 1966.

Jones, A. Philip. *Britain's Search for Chinese Cooperation in the First World War.* New York: Garland Publishing, 1986.

Johnstone, William Crane, Jr. *The Shanghai Problem.* Stanford, Calif.: Stanford University Press, 1937.

King, Frank H.H. *Eastern Banking: Essays in the History of the Hongkong and Shanghai Banking Corporation.* London: The Athlone Press, 1983.

_____. *The Hongkong Bank Between the Wars and the Bank Interned, 1919–1945: Return from Grandeur.* Cambridge: Cambridge University Press, 1988.

King, Paul. *In the Chinese Customs Service: A Personal Record of Forty-Seven Years.* London: Heath Cranton Ltd., 1930.

Kirby, William C. *Germany and Republican China.* Stanford, Calif.: Stanford University Press, 1984.

Ku, Hung-ting. *Urban Mass Movement in Action: The May Thirtieth Movement in Shanghai.* Singapore: Institute of Humanities and Social Sciences Occasional Paper Series, Nanyang University, 1977.

Lee, En-han. *China's Recovery of the British Kiukiang and Hankow Concessions in 1927*. n.p.: University of Western Australia Centre for Far Eastern Studies, n.d.

Levenson, Joseph R. *Confucian China and its Modern Fate: A Trilogy*. Berkeley, Calif.: University of California Press, 1958; 1964; 1965.

Lilley, Charles R., and Michael R. Hunt. "On Social History, the State, and Foreign Relations: Commentary on 'The Cosmopolitan Connection'." *Diplomatic History* vol. 11 no. 3 (Summer 1987), pp. 243-250.

Lo, Hui-min. *Foreign Office Confidential Papers Relating to China and her Neighbouring Countries 1840–1914, with an Additional List 1915-1937*. Paris: Mouton et C$^{ie}$, 1969.

Louis, Wm. Roger. *British Strategy in the Far East 1919–1939*. Oxford: Clarendon Press, 1971.

_____, ed. *Imperialism: The Robinson and Gallagher Controversy*. New York: New Viewpoints, 1976.

Lowe, Peter. *Britain in the Far East: A Survey from 1819 to the Present*. London: Longman, 1981.

McElderry, Andrea Lee. *Shanghai Old-Style Banks (ch'ien-chuang) 1800–1935: A Traditional Institution in a Changing Society*. Ann Arbor, Mich.: Center for Chinese Studies, The University of Michigan, 1976.

_____. "Robber Barons or National Capitalists: Shanghai Bankers in Republican China." *Republican China* vol. 11 no. 1 (November 1985), pp. 52-67.

MacPherson, Kerrie L., and Clifton K. Yearley. "The 2½% Margin: Britain's Shanghai Traders and China's Resilience in the Face of Commercial Penetration." *Journal of Oriental Studies* vol. 25 no. 2 (April 1987), pp 202-234.

Marshall, Jonathan. "Opium and the Politics of Gangsterism in Nationalist China, 1927–45." *Bulletin of Concerned Asian Scholars* vol. 8 no. 3 (July-September 1976), pp. 19-48.

May, Ernest R., and John King Fairbank eds. *America's China Trade in Historical Perspective; The Chinese and American Performance.* Cambridge, Mass.: The Committee on American-East Asian Relations of the Department of History in collaboration with the Council on East Asian Studies, Harvard University; Harvard University Press, 1986.

Metzger, Thomas A. *Escape from Predicament: Neo-Confucianism and China's Evolving Political Culture.* New York: Columbia University Press, 1977.

Miners, Norman. *Hong Kong under Imperial Rule, 1912–1941.* Hong Kong: Oxford University Press, 1987.

Mommsen, Wolfgang J., and Jurgen Osterhammel eds. *Imperialism and After: Continuities and Discontinuities.* London: The German Historical Institute; Allen and Unwin, 1986.

Morse, Hosea Ballou. *The Gilds of China: With an Account of the Gild Merchant or Co-hong of Canton.* Taipei: Ch'eng-wen Publishing Co., 1966.

Murphey, Rhoads M. *Shanghai: Key to Modern China.* Cambridge, Mass.: Harvard University Press, 1953.

_____. *The Outsiders.* Ann Arbor, Mich.: Center for Chinese Studies, The University of Michigan: University of Michigan Press, 1977.

Nathan, Andrew J. *Peking Politics, 1918–1923: Factionalism and the Failure of Constitutionalism.* Berkeley, Calif.: University of California Press, 1976.

_____. *Chinese Democracy.* Berkeley, Calif.: University of California Press, 1985.

Nish, Ian ed. *Some Foreign Attitudes to Republican China: papers by Taichiro Mitani, David Steeds, Ann Trotter, Dudley Cheke.* London: International Centre for Economics and Related Disciplines, London School of Economics, n.d.

Orchard, John E. "Shanghai." *The Geographical Review* no. 26 (1936), pp. 1-31.

Osterhammel, Jürgen. *Britischer Imperialismus im Fernen Osten: Strukturen der Durchdringung und einheimischer Widerstand auf dem chinesischen Markt, 1932–37.* Bochum: Studienverlag Brockmeyer, 1983.

_____. "Imperialism in Transition: British Business and the Chinese Authorities, 1931–1937." *The China Quarterly* vol. 98 (June 1984), pp. 260-286.

*Papers Relating to the Chinese Maritime Customs 1860–1943.* London: School of Oriental and African Studies, 1973.

Pelcovits, Nathan A. *Old China Hands and the Foreign Office.* New York: American Institute of Foreign Relations; King's Crown Press, 1948.

Pollard, Robert T. *China's Foreign Relations 1917–1931.* New York: The Macmillan Co., 1933.

Public Record Office. *The Records of the Foreign Office, 1782–1939.* London: Her Majesty's Stationery Office, 1969.

Ransome, Arthur. *The Chinese Puzzle.* London: George Allen and Unwin, 1927.

Remer, C. F. *A Study of Chinese Boycotts with Special Reference to their Economic Effectiveness.* Baltimore: The Johns Hopkins Press, 1933.

_____. *Foreign Investments in China.* New York: The Macmillan Co., 1933.

*Report of the Hon. Richard Feetham, C.M.G. to the Shanghai Municipal Council.* Shanghai: North-China Daily News and Herald, 1931.

Rhoads, Edward J.M. *China's Republican Revolution: The Case of Kwangtung, 1895–1913.* Cambridge, Mass.: Harvard University Press, 1975.

Rigby, Richard W. *The May 30 Movement: Events and Themes.* Canberra: Australian National University Press, 1980.

Schwarcz, Vera. *The Chinese Enlightenment: Intellectuals and the Legacy of the May Fourth Movement of 1919.* Berkeley, Calif.: University of California Press, 1986.

Seagrave, Sterling. *The Soong Dynasty.* New York: Harper and Row, 1985.

Sergeant, Harriet. *Shanghai: Collision Point of Cultures, 1918/1939.* New York: Crown Publishers, 1990.

Shai, Aron. *Britain and China, 1941–47: Imperial Momentum.* New York: St. Martin's Press, 1984.

"The Shanghai Boom." *Fortune* vol. 11 no. 1 (January 1935), pp. 30-40; 99-120.

Sheridan, James E. *China in Disintegration: The Republican Era in Chinese History 1912–1949.* New York: The Free Press, 1975.

Soothill, W.E. *China and England.* London: Oxford University Press, 1928.

Spence, Jonathan. *To Change China: Western Advisors in China 1620–1960.* New York: Penguin, 1980.

_____. *The Search for Modern China.* New York: W. W. Norton and Company, 1990.

Stremski, Richard. "Britain and Warlordism in China: Relations with Feng Yü-hsiang, 1921–1928." *Journal of Oriental Studies* vol. 11 no. 1 (January 1973), pp. 91-106.

_____. *The Shaping of British Policy during the Nationalist Revolution in China.* Taipei: Soochow University Department of Political Science, 1979.

Tamagna, Frank M. *Banking and Finance in China.* New York: Institute of Pacific Relations, 1942.

T'ang, Leang-li. *China in Revolt: How a Civilisation Became a Nation.* London: Noel Douglas, 1927.

Teichman, Sir Eric. *Affairs of China: A Survey of the Recent History and Present Circumstances of the Republic of China.* London: Methuen, 1938.

Thorne, Christopher. "The Shanghai Crisis of 1932: The Basis of British Policy." *American Historical Review* no. 75 (1970), pp. 1616-1639.

Trotter, Ann. "Backstage Diplomacy: Britian [sic] and Japan in the 1930's." *Journal of Oriental Studies* vol. 15 no. 1 (January 1977), pp. 37-45.

Tyler, W. F. *Pulling Strings in China.* London: Constable & Co. Ltd., 1929.

Vincent, John Carter. *The Extraterritorial System in China: Final Phase.* East Asia Research Center, Harvard University. Cambridge, Mass.: Harvard University Press, 1970.

Wang, Chi. *Endphase des Britischen Kolonialismus in China: eine Untersuchung zur Rolle der öffentlichen Meinung in Grossbrittanien aus Reaktion und Einflussgrüsse britischer Aussenpolitik gegenüber China während der nationalen Revolution 1922–1928.* Frankfurt am Main: P. Lang, 1982.

Wang, Y.C. "Tu Yüeh-sheng (1888–1951): A Tentative Political Biography." *Journal of Asian Studies* vol. 26 (May 1967), pp. 433-455.

Wasserstein, Bernard. *The Secret Lives of Trebitsch Lincoln.* New Haven: Yale University Press, 1988.

Wei, Betty Peh-ti. *Shanghai: Crucible of Modern China.* Hong Kong: Oxford University Press, 1987.

Willert, Sir Arthur. *Aspects of British Foreign Policy.* New Haven: Institute of Politics; Yale University Press, 1928.

Whyte, Sir Frederick. *China and Foreign Powers: A Historical Review of their Relations.*London: Oxford University Press, 1928.

Wilbur, C. Martin. *The Nationalist Revolution in China 1923–1928.* Cambridge: Cambridge University Press, 1983.

Wilgus, Mary H. *Sir Claude MacDonald, the Open Door, and British Informal Empire in China 1895–1900.* New York: Garland Publishing, 1987.

Willoughby, Westel W. *China at the Conference: A Report.* Baltimore, Md.: The Johns Hopkins Press, 1922.

_____. *Constitutional Government in China: Present Conditions and Prospects.* Washington, D. C.: Carnegie Endowment for International Peace, 1922.

_____. *Foreign Rights and Investments in China.* Baltimore: The Johns Hopkins Press, 1927.

Woodhead, H.G.W. "Shanghai and Hong Kong: A British View." *Foreign Affairs* vol. 23 no.2 (January 1945), pp. 295-307.

Wright, Mary Clabaugh. *The Last Stand of Chinese Conservatism: The T'ung-Chih Restoration, 1862–1874.* New York: Atheneum, 1966.

_____, ed. *China in Revolution: The First Phase, 1900–1913.* New Haven: Yale University Press, 1968.

Wright, Stanley F. *The Collection and Disposal of the Maritime and Native Customs Revenue since the Revolution of 1911, with an Account of the Loan Services administered by the Inspector General of Customs (2nd. ed.).* Shanghai: Statistical Department of the Inspectorate General of Customs, 1927.

_____, and John H. Cubbon. *China's Customs Revenue since the Revolution of 1911.* Shanghai: Statistical Department of the Inspectorate General of Customs, 1935.

_____. *China's Struggle for Tariff Autonomy: 1843–1938.* Shanghai: Kelly and Walsh, 1938.

_____. *Hart and the Chinese Customs.* Belfast: Wm. Mullan and Son, 1950.

Young, Arthur N. *China's Nation-Building Effort, 1927–1937: The Financial and Economic Record.* Stanford, Calif.: Hoover Institution Press, Stanford University, 1971.

Zhang, Yongjin. *China in the International System, 1918–1920: The Middle Kingdom at the Periphery.* New York: St. Martin's Press, 1991.

# CORNELL EAST ASIA SERIES

No. 75 *Barbed Wire and Rice: Poems and Songs from Japanese Prisoner-of-War Camps,* collected by Bishop D. McKendree

For ordering information, please contact the Cornell East Asia Series, East Asia Program, Cornell University, 140 Uris Hall, Ithaca, NY 14853-7601, USA; phone (607) 255-6222, fax (607) 255-1388.

2-95/.2M cloth/.5M paper/TS